THE BOOK OF

CURRIES
&
INDIAN FOODS

T H E   B O O K   O F

CURRIES
&
INDIAN FOODS

LINDA FRASER

Photography by
Alister Thorpe

HPBooks

ANOTHER BEST-SELLING VOLUME FROM HPBOOKS

HPBOOKS
Published by The Berkley Publishing Group
200 Madison Avenue
New York, NY 10016

9 8 7 6 5

By arrangement with Salamander Books Ltd., and Merehurst Press, London.

© Salamander Books Ltd., 1989

This book was created by Merehurst Limited
Ferry House, 51-57 Lacy Road, Putney, London SW15

Designer: Roger Daniels
Home Economist: Linda Fraser
Photographer: Alister Thorpe
Color separation: Magnum Graphics Limited
Printed in Belgium by Proost International Book Production

Library of Congress Cataloging-in-Publication Date

Fraser, Linda
    The book of curries & Indian foods
    Includes index.
    ISBN 0-89586-820-2
    1. Cookery, India.   2. Cookery (Curry)   I. Title.
TX724.5.I4F73   1989   89-1811
641.5954   CIP

CONTENTS

INTRODUCTION

Indian food is rich and varied; it includes many regional cooking styles—each highly distinctive, but all equally delicious.

The Book of Curries & Indian Foods dips into all the regions to bring you over 100 recipes—all beautifully illustrated in color with step-by-step instructions. Discover how to transform everyday foods into exotic dishes—from the well-known Chicken Tikka to Sole with Dill Stuffing and Golden Steamed Chicken.

You'll discover the rich variety of Indian vegetable dishes, too. Ordinary vegetables are transformed when combined with wonderful spices and delicious sauces.

Find out the secrets of Indian breads like Chapati and Naan—there are easy-to-follow recipes with step-by-step instructions to make them simple to prepare.

You will find that not all Indian food is hot—there are mouthwatering salads, fresh chutneys and fabulous, irresistible desserts, such as Fritters & Fragrant Syrup and Pistachio Halva, that are sweet and delicately scented, as well as cooling fruity summer drinks like Lime & Mint Drink and Indian Summer Punch.

When you try the recipes, remember that they are only meant as a basic guide—add a pinch of extra spice here, omit the chiles there or add an extra ingredient if you like. It's your personal touch—what the Indians call *Hath ki bat*—that makes all the difference!

CULTURAL INFLUENCES

Indian Food encompasses the cooking of many different regions —the country itself is huge, over a million square miles—and the foods are quite different from state to state. Geography and local produce both play a part in forming the diverse regional traditions.

In the north, where the climate is temperate, sheep are reared—and the dishes are generally cooked slowly in the oven. Travelling south through Dehli and the Punjab, the diet becomes much richer—here they cook mainly with ghee (a clarified butter) and eat both goat and chicken. In these northern regions, instead of rice, the preference is for breads such as chapatis and parathas.

To the east around the Bay of Bengal, there is an abundance of fish from the many rivers and, of course, from the bay itself. Coconut palms grow in the hot and humid climate, so coconut also features strongly in many of their recipes. On the west coast, in Gujarat, the people are mainly vegetarian, eating lots of beans and peas as well as vegetables and in Tamil Nadu in the far southeast, the people are also vegetarian.

The humid tropical conditions of the southwest, in Goa and Malabar, mean that date and coconut palms, and banana plants flourish. Here there is also plenty of fish and shellfish. Southern Indians eat more rice than the northerners and they prefer to steam foods—the dishes are traditionally very hot, much more so than in the north.

Influence of Race & Religion
India is a country of vastly varied races and religions—and it is religion that influences diet to the greatest extent. There are hundreds of different religions, some original, others imported over the centuries by conquering peoples from other lands, each with its own customs and taboos. For instance, Moslems and Jews don't eat pork, while Hindus and Sikhs are prohibited from eating beef—and although many Hindus are strict vegetarians, others eat fish and shellfish,

classing these as a harvest from the seas. The taboos don't just cover meats—Kashmiri Hindus also don't eat onions or garlic, or vegetables or fruit that resemble meaty colors such as beets, tomatoes or watermelon.

Use of Spices

The imaginative use of spices sets Indian cooking apart from other cuisines—it is by far the most aromatic of all types of cooking—and perhaps the most pleasant discovery one can make about it is that although always spicy, the food isn't necessarily hot. In fact, chiles—which make the food hot—were only introduced to India in the 16th century.

Red chiles are milder than green, and larger chiles generally milder than small ones and unless you like very hot food, the seeds of all types are best removed. Be careful when handling chiles and always wash your hands afterward to prevent irritation.

Other spices can add warmth in different degrees—mustard seeds, black pepper and cayenne pepper are all quite hot, while ground ginger, nutmeg and cardamom are warm. Warm and hot spices feature more in the winter months because they generate heat in the body, while the cooler spices such as fennel, cloves and green cardamom are used in summer drinks and desserts.

The cornerstone of Indian cooking is the spice mixtures—or masalas. Spices release their flavor when they are crushed and traditionally the spices are ground by hand on a grinding stone with a pestle. At home, a mortar and pestle works very well for small quantities. However, if you have an electric coffee grinder, you will be able to make spice grinding easy.

The most common spices are cumin, coriander seeds and mustard seeds, black pepper, ground turmeric, cinnamon, cardamom and cloves. Whole spices have a more intense flavor that lasts much longer. Buy small quantities and store them in an airtight container in a cool place. Whole spices will stay fresh from one to three years, while ground spices are really fresh for up to three months.

− SPICE MIXES & COCONUT MILK −

NUT MASALA
2 tablespoons vegetable oil
1 teaspoon cumin seeds
1 teaspoon cardamom seeds
1 tablespoon poppy seeds
1 teaspoon black peppercorns
2 garlic cloves, crushed
1 (1-inch) piece fresh gingerroot, grated
2 oz. blanched almonds or unsalted cashew nuts,
    chopped
1/4 cup boiling water

Heat oil in a heavy skillet, add spices and cook over medium heat 5 to 10 minutes, until golden brown, stirring constantly. Add garlic and gingerroot and cook 2 minutes more, then cool.

Put spice mixture in a blender or food processor fitted with the metal blade. Add almonds or cashew nuts and water; grind to a smooth paste. Cover tightly and keep in a cool place for up to 1 month.

TANDOORI MASALA
1 tablespoon cumin seeds
1 tablespoon coriander seeds
1 tablespoon red (cayenne) pepper
Few drops of red food coloring

Grind cumin and coriander seeds to a fine powder in a coffee grinder or with a pestle and mortar. Stir in cayenne and food coloring and mix well. Store in a small airtight jar up to 2 months.

MOGHUL MASALA

Seeds from 2 oz. (1/4 cup) green cardamom pods
2 (3-inch) cinnamon sticks, crushed
1 tablespoon whole cloves
1 tablespoon black peppercorns
1 teaspoon grated nutmeg

Grind spices to a fine powder in a coffee grinder or with a pestle and mortar. Store in a small, airtight jar up to 2 months.

GARAM MASALA

1 tablespoon plus 1 teaspoon cardamom seeds
2 (3-inch) cinnamon sticks, crushed
2 teaspoons whole cloves
1 tablespoon plus 1 teaspoon black peppercorns
3 tablespoons cumin seeds
3 tablespoons coriander seeds

Put all spices in a heavy skillet and dry roast over medium heat 5 to 10 minutes, until browned, stirring constantly. Cool completely, then grind to a fine powder in a coffee grinder or with a pestle and mortar. Store in an airtight jar up to 2 months.

HOT SPICE MIX

1/4 cup cumin seeds
8 dried red chiles
1 tablespoon black peppercorns
1 tablespoon cardamom seeds
1 (3-inch) cinnamon stick, crushed
1 tablespoon plus 1 teaspoon black mustard seeds
1 tablespoon fenugreek seeds

Put all spices in a heavy skillet and dry roast over medium heat 5 to 10 minutes, until browned, stirring constantly. Cool completely, then grind to a fine powder in a coffee grinder or with a pestle and mortar. Store in an airtight jar up to 2 months.

COCONUT MILK

1 cup dried shredded coconut
2 cups hot water

Put coconut and water in a blender or food processor fitted with the metal blade; process 1 minute. Strain through a fine sieve, pressing out as much liquid as possible, then discard coconut.

Makes about 2 cups.

Note: Substitute grated fresh coconut for dried coconut, if preferred. Or mix powdered coconut milk according to package directions. Canned coconut milk is also available.

Murghal Masala Chops

8 lamb loin chops
1 tablespoon Murghal Masala, page 11
1/4 teaspoon chile powder
1 garlic clove, crushed
1 tablespoon lemon juice
Chicory and cherry tomatoes, to garnish

Wipe lamb chops with a damp paper towel; trim off any excess fat. Slash meaty parts two or three times on each side and set aside.

Put Murghal Masala, chile powder, garlic and lemon juice in a small bowl; mix to a smooth paste. Rub paste into chops, cover and refrigerate 2 to 3 hours to allow meat to absorb flavors.

Preheat broiler or grill. Place chops on a grill rack and cook 12 to 15 minutes, until browned on outside and just pink in center, turning over halfway through cooking. Press point of a sharp knife into center of chops— when they are ready, juices will be just faintly pink. Serve hot, garnished with chicory and tomatoes.

Makes 4 servings.

Skewered Beef Kabobs

1-1/2 pounds lean ground beef
1 onion, finely chopped
1 (2-inch) piece fresh gingerroot, grated
3 garlic cloves, crushed
1 teaspoon chile powder
1 tablespoon Garam Masala, page 11
1 tablespoon chopped cilantro (fresh coriander)
1 tablespoon ground almonds
1 egg, beaten
1/4 cup garbanzo bean flour
6 tablespoons plain yogurt
2 teaspoons vegetable oil
Onion rings and thin lemon wedges, to garnish

Mix together beef, onion, gingerroot, garlic, spices, cilantro, almonds, egg and flour in a large bowl. Cover beef mixture and refrigerate up to 4 hours to allow flavors to blend. Shape into 16 to 20 long ovals; thread onto four long skewers. Mix together yogurt and oil and brush over kabobs.

Preheat broiler or grill. Cook kabobs 20 to 25 minutes, until well browned and no longer pink in center. Baste kabobs with more of the yogurt and oil mixture and turn occasionally during cooking. Serve hot, garnished with onion rings and lemon wedges.

Makes 4 servings.

Note: The meatball mixture can be made up to 12 hours in advance and refrigerated.

Lamb Tikka

1 (2-lb.) boneless leg of lamb
1 teaspoon ground cumin
3/4 teaspoon ground turmeric
Salt to taste
6 tablespoons plain yogurt
1/2 small onion, finely chopped
1 (2-inch) piece fresh gingerroot, grated
2 garlic cloves, crushed
Few drops red food coloring, optional
1 teaspoon Garam Masala, page 11

Trim fat from lamb; cut lamb into 1-1/2-inch cubes. Put lamb cubes in a bowl; add cumin, turmeric, salt, yogurt, onion, gingerroot and garlic.

Mix together well, then, if you wish, add enough coloring to give mixture a red tint. Cover and refrigerate 4 to 6 hours. Drain lamb from marinade and thread cubes onto eight short skewers, pressing cubes closely together.

Preheat broiler or grill. Cook kabobs 15 to 20 minutes, or until done, basting kabobs with any remaining marinade and turning occasionally during cooking. The lamb is ready when it is browned on the outside and still slightly pink in the center. Sprinkle with Garam Masala and serve at once.

Makes 4 servings.

Kashmir Meatball Curry

1-1/2 pounds ground lamb
1/4 cup garbanzo bean flour
3 tablespoons Garam Masala, page 11
1/4 teaspoon red (cayenne) pepper
Salt to taste
6 tablespoons plain yogurt
2 tablespoons vegetable oil
1 (3-inch) cinnamon stick
6 green cardamom pods, bruised
2 fresh bay leaves
6 whole cloves
1 (2-inch) piece fresh gingerroot, grated
1 cup water
2 tablespoons chopped cilantro (fresh
    coriander), to garnish

Put lamb, flour, Garam Masala, cayenne, salt and half the yogurt in a bowl; mix together well. Shape into 16 long ovals. Heat oil in a shallow heavy saucepan, add cinnamon, cardamom pods, bay leaves and cloves. Stir-fry a few seconds, then add meatballs; cook until lightly browned on all sides. Add gingerroot; cook a few seconds more. Stir remaining yogurt into water; pour over meatballs.

Cover pan and bring to a boil. Reduce heat and simmer about 30 minutes, until meatballs are cooked and almost all the sauce has been absorbed, stirring gently two or three times. Sprinkle with cilantro and serve at once.

Makes 4 servings.

Note: If meatballs release a lot of fat during initial cooking, drain off fat before adding yogurt liquid.

Hot & Sour Pork Curry

1-1/2 pounds boneless shoulder of pork
6 tablespoons vegetable oil
2 onions, thinly sliced
3 tablespoons Hot Spice Mix, page 11
1/4 cup white wine vinegar
1 teaspoon brown sugar
1 (1-inch) piece fresh gingerroot, grated
6 garlic cloves, crushed
1 teaspoon ground turmeric
1 teaspoon paprika
1 teaspoon ground coriander
1 cup water
Red chile flower, to garnish

Wipe pork with a damp paper towel; cut into 1-inch cubes.

Heat half the oil in a heavy saucepan, add onions and cook 10 minutes, or until brown and crisp, stirring all the time. Remove with a slotted spoon and set aside. Mix together spice mix, vinegar, sugar, gingerroot, garlic, turmeric, paprika and coriander in a small bowl, blending to a smooth paste. Add remaining oil to pan; add pork and cook until lightly browned, remove with a slotted spoon and set aside.

Add spice mixture to pan; cook, stirring, a few minutes. Return meat and any juices to pan. Stir in water. Bring to a boil. Reduce heat, cover and simmer 45 minutes. Stir in three-quarters of the onions and cook another 20 to 30 minutes, until pork is tender. Serve hot, garnished with remaining onions and chile flower.

Makes 4 servings.

Red Lamb & Almond Curry

1-1/2 pounds boneless leg of lamb
1/4 cup vegetable oil
1 large onion, finely chopped
6 green cardamom pods, bruised
1 teaspoon ground turmeric
1 teaspoon chile powder
1 teaspoon ground cumin
1 tablespoon paprika
1 teaspoon ground coriander
1 recipe Nut Masala, made with almonds, page 10
2/3 cup plain yogurt
1 (14-oz.) can chopped tomatoes

Trim excess fat from lamb; cut lamb into 1-1/2-inch cubes. Heat oil in a heavy saucepan; add onion. Cook until softened; add cardamom, turmeric, chile powder, cumin, paprika, coriander and masala. Cook, stirring, 2 to 3 minutes, then stir in yogurt and tomatoes and bring to a boil. Add lamb cubes and stir well.

Bring to a boil, then reduce heat, cover and cook 40 to 50 minutes, until lamb is tender and liquid makes a thick sauce, stirring occasionally.

Makes 4 servings.

Note: On special occasions, this dish can be garnished with real silver leaf which can be bought, in thin sheets on backing paper, from Indian shops. Just before serving, place a sheet of foil, silver side down, on top of the curry and peel off the backing paper.

Lamb Korma

1-1/2 pounds boneless leg of lamb
1/4 cup vegetable oil
1 large onion, finely chopped
1 recipe Nut Masala, made with cashews, page
    10
2 tablespoons Garam Masala, page 11
3 dried red chiles, seeded, crushed
1 (1-inch) piece fresh gingerroot, grated
1 tablespoon chopped cilantro (fresh coriander)
1 cup half and half
1/3 cup water
Salt to taste
2 teaspoons lemon juice
Cilantro (fresh coriander) leaves and lemon
    wedges, to garnish

Wipe lamb with a damp paper towel, trim off
excess fat and cut lamb into 2-inch cubes.

Heat oil in a heavy saucepan, add lamb and
cook until browned all over. Add onion and
cook about 5 minutes to soften, stirring frequently. Stir in masalas, chiles and gingerroot; cook 2 minutes more.

Add chopped cilantro, half and half, water
and salt. Bring to a boil. Reduce heat, cover
and simmer about 1 hour, or until lamb is
tender. Stir in lemon juice. Serve hot, garnished with cilantro and lemon wedges.

Makes 4 servings.

Madras Meat Curry

1-1/2 pounds beef round steak
2 tablespoons vegetable oil
1 large onion, finely sliced
4 whole cloves
4 green cardamom pods, bruised
3 green chiles, seeded, finely chopped
2 dry red chiles, seeded, crushed
1 (1-inch) piece fresh gingerroot, grated
2 garlic cloves, crushed
2 teaspoons ground coriander
2 teaspoons ground turmeric
1/4 cup water
1/4 cup tamarind nectar, see note below
Salt to taste
Lettuce leaves, to garnish

Cut beef into 1-inch cubes. Heat oil in a large heavy saucepan, add beef and cook until browned all over. Remove with a slotted spoon and set aside. Add onion, cloves and cardamom to pan; cook, stirring, about 8 minutes, until onion is soft and golden brown. Stir in chiles, gingerroot, garlic, coriander and turmeric; cook 2 minutes. Return beef to pan, add water and cover. Simmer 1 hour.

Stir in tamarind nectar and salt; simmer another 20 to 30 minutes, until beef is tender. Serve, garnished with lettuce leaves.

Makes 4 servings.

Note: Tamarind nectar: soak a walnut-sized piece of tamarind paste in 1 cup boiling water about 20 minutes, then squeeze in cheesecloth to extract liquid, discard pulp. Store in refrigerator up to 1 week. Tamarind nectar is also available commercially.

Minty Minced Lamb Patties

1/3 cup whole brown lentils
1-1/4 cups boiling water
3 onions, finely chopped
1 pound ground lamb
2 tablespoons Garam Masala, page 11
2 dried red chiles, seeded, crushed
1 egg, beaten
1/4 cup plain yogurt
2 tablespoons chopped fresh mint
2 green chiles, seeded, chopped
1/4 cup vegetable oil
Lettuce and fresh mint leaves, to garnish

Put lentils in a bowl, add water and leave to soak 2 hours.

Put lentils, their soaking water, 2 onions, lamb, Garam Masala and red chiles in a large heavy saucepan and bring to a boil. Cook over medium heat until all the liquid has evaporated and mixture is very dry, stirring constantly. Remove from heat; cool. Put mixture in a blender or food processor fitted with the metal blade; process to a smooth paste. Add egg and yogurt and blend again. Cover and refrigerate 2 to 3 hours, then form into 16 balls.

Mix together remaining onion, mint and green chiles. Make an indentation in each lamb ball and stuff with a little mint mixture, then cover up with meat. Flatten balls into 2-inch rounds. Heat oil in a skillet; add patties a few at a time. Cook 4 to 6 minutes, until well browned, turning over after 2 to 3 minutes. Serve, garnished with lettuce and mint.

Makes 4 servings.

Roast Lamb & Pistachios

1 (3-1/2- to 4-lb.) leg of lamb, boned, rolled and
   tied
2 garlic cloves, crushed
1 (1-inch) piece fresh gingerroot, grated
1 teaspoon ground cumin
2 teaspoons Murghal Masala, page 11
Salt and red (cayenne) pepper to taste
3/4 cup shelled pistachios
2 tablespoons lemon juice
2 tablespoons brown sugar
1/2 cup plain yogurt
2/3 cup water
2 pinches saffron threads
2 tablespoons boiling water
1 tablespoon cornstarch
2 tablespoons shelled pistachios, sliced, to
   garnish

Prick lamb all over with point of a knife, place
in a large non-metal casserole dish. Put garlic,
gingerroot, cumin, Murghal Masala, salt,
cayenne, pistachios, lemon juice, sugar and
yogurt in a blender or food processor fitted
with the metal blade; process until smooth.
Pour over lamb. Cover and refrigerate 24
hours, turning lamb occasionally. Preheat
oven to 350F (175C). Add water to lamb;
bring to a boil.

Cover tightly and cook in oven 1-1/2 hours.
Reduce heat to 300F (150C); cook another 30
minutes. Turn off oven and leave 30 minutes.
Meanwhile soak saffron in boiling water 20
minutes, then blend in cornstarch. Remove
lamb and keep warm. Skim excess fat from
sauce; pour sauce into a saucepan. Add saffron mixture; cook, stirring, until boiling and
thickened. Slice lamb, pour a little sauce over
and garnish with pistachios. Serve remaining
sauce separately.

Makes 6 to 8 servings.

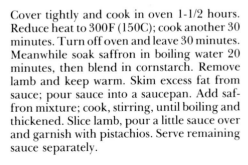

Beef-Stuffed Cabbage

2 onions
5 tablespoons vegetable oil
3 garlic cloves, crushed
2 green chiles, seeded, chopped
1 (3-inch) piece fresh gingerroot, grated
1 pound ground beef
1/4 teaspoon ground turmeric
2 teaspoons Garam Masala, page 11
1 savoy cabbage
1 (14-oz.) can chopped tomatoes
2 tablespoons lemon juice
Salt and pepper to taste
2/3 cup water
Lemon slices, to garnish

Chop 1 onion and slice the other. Heat 2 tablespoons oil in a heavy saucepan, add chopped onion and cook, stirring, over medium heat about 8 minutes, until soft and golden brown. Add garlic, chiles and one-third of the gingerroot; cook 1 minute, then remove with a slotted spoon and set aside. Add beef to pan and cook, stirring, until browned and well broken up. Stir in turmeric and Garam Masala, cook 1 minute, then add onion mixture.

Cover and cook 20 to 30 minutes, stirring occasionally, until cooking liquid is absorbed; cool. Remove core from cabbage with a sharp knife. Cook whole cabbage in boiling salted water 8 minutes, then drain and rinse in cold water. Leave until cool enough to handle, then carefully peel off 12 to 16 outside leaves, keeping them whole. Finely shred rest of cabbage.

Make sauce, heat remaining oil in a heavy saucepan, add sliced onion and cook, stirring frequently, 5 minutes, or until soft, but not brown. Add shredded cabbage, tomatoes, remaining gingerroot, lemon juice, salt, pepper and water. Bring to a boil and simmer 5 minutes.

Preheat oven to 375F (190C). Put about 2 tablespoons beef mixture on each cabbage leaf, fold sides in and roll up neatly. Pour a little sauce into bottom of a casserole dish, add cabbage rolls and pour over rest of sauce. Cover and bake 40 to 50 minutes, until cabbage is tender. Serve hot, garnished with lemon slices.

Makes 4 servings.

Lamb with Onions

1-1/2 pounds lamb shoulder
1 teaspoon ground turmeric
1 teaspoon ground cumin
1 teaspoon ground coriander
1 (1-inch) piece fresh gingerroot, grated
2 garlic cloves, crushed
3 tablespoons vegetable oil
1 tablespoon superfine sugar
4 large onions, sliced into thin rings
1 lb. potatoes, cut into large chunks
1 cup water
Salt and red (cayenne) pepper to taste
1 teaspoon Garam Masala, page 11
Rosemary sprigs, to garnish

Wipe lamb with a damp paper towel, trim off excess fat and cut into 1-1/2-inch cubes.

Put lamb in a non-metal bowl. Mix together turmeric, cumin, coriander, gingerroot and garlic; add to lamb. Stir well, then cover loosely and refrigerate 2 to 3 hours. Heat oil in a heavy saucepan until smoking. Stir in sugar, then add onions and cook over medium-high heat 10 minutes, until a rich brown, stirring frequently. Remove onions with a slotted spoon and set aside.

Add lamb to pan; cook until browned all over. Add potatoes and cook, stirring, 2 minutes. Return onions to pan; add water, salt and cayenne. Bring to a boil. Reduce heat, cover and simmer 1-1/4 hours, or until lamb is tender, stirring occasionally. Stir in Garam Masala and serve, garnished with rosemary sprigs.

Makes 4 servings.

Spicy Spareribs

2-1/2 pounds meaty pork spareribs
3 tablespoons Hot Spice Mix, page 11
1 teaspoon ground turmeric
1 (2-inch) piece fresh gingerroot, grated
1 small onion, finely chopped
1 tablespoon white wine vinegar
1 tablespoon tomato paste
5 tablespoons water
Green onions and tomato wedges, to garnish

Cut ribs into single rib pieces; chop ribs into 3-inch lengths.

Place ribs in a large saucepan, cover with cold water and bring to a boil. Reduce heat and simmer 15 minutes, then drain. Put spice mix, turmeric, gingerroot, onion, vinegar, tomato paste and water in a blender or food processor fitted with the metal blade; process until smooth.

Place ribs in a non-metal bowl, add spice mixture and stir to coat well. Cover and refrigerate 2 to 3 hours. Transfer ribs to a broiler pan. Preheat broiler; cook about 15 minutes, until well browned and very tender, turning occasionally and basting with any remaining marinade. Serve hot, garnished with onions and tomatoes.

Makes 4 servings.

Pork in Spinach Sauce

1-1/2 pounds fresh spinach
Salt to taste
1-1/2 pounds lean boneless pork
3 tablespoons vegetable oil
2 onions, finely sliced
4 garlic cloves, crushed
1 (1-inch) piece fresh gingerroot, grated
3 tablespoons Garam Masala, page 11
1/2 teaspoon ground turmeric
1 bay leaf
2 tomatoes, peeled, chopped
2 green chiles, seeded, chopped
2/3 cup plain yogurt
1-2/3 cups water
Sliced tomato and bay leaves, to garnish

Trim stems from spinach and cook leaves in boiling salted water 2 to 3 minutes until tender. Drain thoroughly and rinse under cold running water. Put in a blender or food processor fitted with the metal blade; process to a smooth puree. Set aside. Preheat oven to 325F (160C). Cut pork into 1-inch cubes. Heat oil in a large skillet and fry pork until browned all over. Transfer to a casserole dish using a slotted spoon.

Add onions to pan and cook, stirring, 10 to 15 minutes, until a rich brown. Add garlic, gingerroot, Garam Masala, turmeric, bay leaf, tomatoes and chiles. Cook, stirring 2 to 3 minutes, until tomatoes are softened. Add yogurt and water and stir well. Pour over pork, cover and bake 1-1/4 to 1-1/2 hours, until pork is tender. Remove bay leaf, stir in spinach and salt, re-cover and bake another 10 minutes. Serve hot, garnished with tomatoes and bay leaves.

Makes 4 servings.

Lamb with Cauliflower

1-1/2 pounds lean lamb
3 tablespoons vegetable oil
2 onions, finely chopped
1 (1-inch) piece fresh gingerroot, grated
4 garlic cloves, crushed
2 tablespoons Hot Spice Mix, page 11
1-1/4 cups beef stock
Salt to taste
1 small cauliflower, cut into flowerets
1 teaspoon Garam Masala, page 11
2 teaspoons lime juice
Lime slices, to garnish

Trim excess fat from lamb; cut into 1-inch cubes. Set aside.

Heat oil in a large heavy saucepan; add onions. Cook over medium heat 5 minutes, until soft, stirring frequently. Stir in gingerroot, garlic and spice mix; cook 1 minute. Add lamb; cook until browned all over.

Stir in stock and salt; bring to a boil. Cover and simmer 25 minutes. Add cauliflowerets; cook another 5 to 10 minutes, until lamb and cauliflower are tender, stirring occasionally. Sprinkle in Garam Masala and lime juice and stir gently. Serve hot, garnished with lime slices.

Makes 4 servings.

Chicken in Ginger Sauce

4 (6-oz.) boneless chicken breasts, skinned
2 tablespoons vegetable oil
6 green onions, finely chopped
3 garlic cloves, crushed
1 (2-inch) piece fresh gingerroot, grated
1 teaspoon ground cumin
2 teaspoons Garam Masala, page 11
Salt and pepper to taste
1 tablespoon lemon juice
6 tablespoons hot water
Parsley sprigs and lemon slice,
   to garnish

Rinse chicken, pat dry with paper towels and slice thinly.

Heat oil in a large skillet, add onions and cook 2 to 3 minutes, to soften, stirring. Remove from pan with a slotted spoon. Add chicken to pan and cook over high heat, stirring frequently, for about 5 minutes, or until browned all over.

Stir in garlic, gingerroot, cumin, Garam Masala, salt and pepper. Cook 1 minute, then stir in cooked onions, lemon juice and water. Cover and cook over low heat about 10 minutes, or until chicken is tender. Serve hot, garnished with parsley and lemon.

Makes 4 servings.

Roast Duck in Fruit Sauce

1 (4-1/2-lb.) duck
3 onions, chopped
1 cup chopped mixed nuts
1 cup fresh bread crumbs
4 tablespoons chopped cilantro (fresh coriander)
Salt and red (cayenne) pepper, to taste
1 egg yolk
1 tablespoon Garam Masala, page 11
2 tablespoons vegetable oil
2 garlic cloves, crushed
1 (1-inch) piece fresh gingerroot, grated
1 teaspoon ground turmeric
2 tablespoons ground coriander
1 teaspoon garbanzo bean flour
1-1/4 cups plain yogurt
Juice of 2 lemons and 2 oranges

Preheat oven to 375F (190C). Rinse duck, pat dry with paper towels, then prick skin with a fork. In a bowl, mix together 1 onion, nuts, bread crumbs, 3 tablespoons cilantro, salt, cayenne pepper and egg yolk. Stuff duck with mixture, then truss neatly. Rub Garam Masala into skin; place duck in a roasting pan. Roast 1-1/4 hours, or until tender, spoon off fat from pan as it accumulates. Remove duck and keep warm. Heat oil in a saucepan, add remaining onions and cook, stirring, 5 minutes, until soft.

Stir in garlic, gingerroot, turmeric, ground coriander, salt, cayenne and flour. Cook 1 minute, then stir in yogurt. Simmer 10 minutes, then stir in lemon juice and orange juice and heat gently, without boiling. Carve duck. Arrange on a platter; pour sauce over duck and sprinkle with remaining 1 tablespoon cilantro. Serve hot.

Makes 4 servings.

Note: This looks very attractive garnished with spirals of orange and lemon peel.

Lemon & Coriander Chicken

4 chicken thighs, skinned
4 chicken drumsticks, skinned
1/4 cup vegetable oil
1 (2-inch) piece fresh gingerroot, grated
4 garlic cloves, crushed
1 green chile, seeded, finely chopped
1/2 teaspoon ground turmeric
1 teaspoon ground cumin
1 teaspoon ground coriander
Salt and red (cayenne) pepper to taste
1/2 cup water
Grated peel and juice of 1 lemon
4 oz. cilantro (fresh coriander), chopped
Cilantro (fresh coriander) leaves and lemon
    slices, to garnish

Rinse chicken; pat dry with paper towels. Heat oil in a large skillet and add chicken. Fry, turning frequently, until browned all over. Remove from pan with a slotted spoon; set aside. Add gingerroot and garlic to skillet; cook 1 minute. Stir in chile, turmeric, cumin, coriander, salt and cayenne; cook 1 minute more.

Return chicken to pan, add water and lemon peel and juice. Bring to a boil, then cover and cook over medium heat 25 to 30 minutes, or until chicken is tender. Stir in chopped cilantro. Serve hot, garnished with cilantro leaves and lemon slices.

Makes 4 servings.

Variation: Substitute fresh parsley, or a mixture of parsley and mint for the cilantro, if preferred.

Apricot & Chicken Curry

2-1/2-lbs. chicken pieces, skinned
1/2 teaspoon chile powder
1 tablespoon Garam Masala, page 11
1 (1-inch) piece fresh gingerroot, grated
2 garlic cloves, crushed
1 cup dried apricots
2/3 cup water
2 tablespoons vegetable oil
2 onions, finely sliced
1 (14-oz.) can chopped tomatoes
Salt to taste
1 tablespoon sugar
2 tablespoons white wine vinegar

Rinse chicken; pat dry with paper towels. Cut each piece into four pieces and put in a large bowl. Add chile powder, Garam Masala, gingerroot and garlic; toss well to coat chicken pieces. Cover and refrigerate 2 to 3 hours to allow chicken to absorb flavors. In a separate bowl, combine apricots and water; soak 2 to 3 hours.

Heat oil in a large heavy saucepan; add chicken pieces. Cook over high heat about 5 minutes, or until browned all over. Remove from pan and set aside. Add onions to pan and cook, stirring, about 5 minutes, until soft. Return chicken to pan with tomatoes, cover and cook over low heat 20 minutes. Drain apricots, add to pan with salt, sugar and vinegar. Simmer, covered, 10 to 15 minutes, until tender. Serve hot.

Makes 4 servings.

Tandoori Chicken

2-1/2 lbs. chicken pieces
1 tablespoon lime juice
Salt to taste
1 small onion
1 tablespoon Tandoori Masala, page 10
2 teaspoons Garam Masala, page 11
1 (1-inch) piece fresh gingerroot, grated
1-1/4 cups plain yogurt
Cilantro (fresh coriander) and lime wedges to
   garnish

Rinse chicken pieces, pat dry with paper towels, then slash meaty parts two or three times.

Place chicken in a shallow non-metal dish. Sprinkle with lime juice and salt. Set aside. Put onion, masalas, gingerroot, salt and yogurt into a blender or food processor fitted with the metal blade; process until smooth and frothy. Pour over chicken and cover loosely. Marinate in the refrigerator 6 hours, or overnight.

Preheat oven to 400F (205C). Drain excess marinade from chicken pieces; place them in a roasting pan. Cook 25 to 30 minutes, until tender and well browned. Serve hot, garnished with cilantro and lime wedges.

Makes 4 servings.

Note: If preferred, use a 3-1/2 pound roasting chicken and cook for about 1-1/4 hours, or until juices run clear, when thigh is pierced with a knife.

Spicy Chicken Patties

1-1/4 lbs. boneless chicken breasts, skinned
4 green onions, finely chopped
3 tomatoes, peeled, seeded, chopped
3 tablespoons chopped cilantro (fresh
    coriander)
1 (1-inch) piece fresh gingerroot, grated
1 garlic clove, crushed
1 teaspoon ground cumin
1 teaspoon Garam Masala, page 11
Salt and red (cayenne) pepper to taste
1 egg, beaten
1-1/2 cups fresh bread crumbs
1/4 cup vegetable oil
Tomato wedges and green onion brushes, to
    garnish

Rinse chicken breasts; pat dry with paper towels. Finely mince chicken and put into a large bowl with onions, tomatoes, cilantro, gingerroot, garlic, cumin, Garam Masala, salt, cayenne, egg and half of the bread crumbs. Mix thoroughly, then divide into 18 pieces and form into patties. Roll patties in remaining bread crumbs, to coat completely.

Heat oil in a large skillet. Fry patties in two or three batches 10 to 12 minutes, until crisp and golden brown and no longer pink in center. Drain on paper towels. Serve hot, garnished with tomato wedges and green onion brushes.

Makes 6 servings.

Variation: Use boneless turkey breast instead of chicken, if preferred.

Note: Patties can be prepared up to 12 hours in advance, chill until ready to cook.

Duck & Coconut Curry

4 (8-oz.) duck quarters, skinned
2 tablespoons vegetable oil
1 teaspoon mustard seeds
1 onion, finely chopped
3 garlic cloves, crushed
1 (2-inch) piece fresh gingerroot, grated
2 green chiles, seeded, chopped
1 teaspoon ground cumin
1 tablespoon ground coriander
1 teaspoon ground turmeric
1 tablespoon white wine vinegar
Salt and red (cayenne) pepper to taste
1-1/4 cups Coconut Milk, page 11
2 tablespoons shredded coconut, toasted, and
  lemon wedges to garnish

Rinse duck; pat dry with paper towels. Heat oil in a large skillet, add duck and cook, turning often over high heat 8 to 10 minutes, until browned all over, then remove from pan. Pour off all but 2 tablespoons fat from pan, add mustard seeds and fry 1 minute, or until they begin to pop.

Add onion to pan and cook, stirring, over medium heat 8 minutes, or until soft and golden. Stir in garlic, gingerroot, chiles, cumin, coriander and turmeric; cook 2 minutes. Stir in vinegar, return duck to pan and turn pieces to coat them in spice mixture. Stir in Coconut Milk and bring to a boil. Cover and cook over low heat about 40 minutes, or until duck is tender and sauce has thickened. Season with salt and cayenne. Serve hot, garnished with shredded coconut and lemon wedges.

Makes 4 servings.

Chicken Biriani

1-1/4 lbs. boneless chicken breasts, skinned
6 tablespoons vegetable oil
6 green cardamom pods, bruised
1/2 teaspoon cumin seeds
2 onions, finely sliced
4 garlic cloves, crushed
1 (2-inch) piece fresh gingerroot, grated
2/3 cup plain yogurt
1/2 cup water
3 cups basmati rice, washed
Salt and ground black pepper to taste
Large pinch of saffron threads
2 tablespoons boiling water
2 tablespoons cold water
Few drops red food coloring
3 tablespoons sliced almonds, toasted, and 2
**   tablespoons raisins, to garnish**

Cut chicken into 3/4-inch cubes. Set aside. Soak rice in cold water 30 minutes, then drain. Heat 4 tablespoons oil in a large heavy saucepan, add cardamom pods and cumin seeds and fry 1 minute. Stir in onions, garlic, gingerroot and chicken; cook about 5 minutes, stirring over high heat, until chicken is browned all over. Stir in yogurt 1 tablespoon at a time, then add 1/2 cup water. Reduce heat, cover and simmer 15 minutes.

Heat remaining oil in a separate pan, stir in rice and fry 2 to 3 minutes, until golden, stirring constantly. Stir into chicken mixture with salt and pepper. Cover and simmer 12 to 15 minutes, until rice and chicken are tender. Soak saffron in boiling water 5 minutes. Add cold water to food coloring. Pour saffron liquid and red mixture into separate 1/3 sections of rice and stir in to color rice yellow and red, leaving 1/3 white. Serve hot, garnished with almonds and raisins.

Makes 4 servings.

Golden Steamed Chicken

1 (3-1/2-lb.) chicken
3/4 cup basmati rice
3 tablespoons vegetable oil
1/2 teaspoon chile powder
1/3 cup raisins
1/2 cup sliced almonds
1 tablespoon chopped fresh thyme
3/4 cup water
Salt to taste
1/2 teaspoon ground cumin
1/2 teaspoon ground turmeric
1 teaspoon ground coriander
2 teaspoons Garam Masala, page 11
Salt and red (cayenne) pepper to taste
1/2 cup hot water
Thyme sprigs, to garnish

Rinse chicken, pat dry with paper towels and
set aside. Wash rice thoroughly and soak in
cold water 30 minutes, then drain. Heat 1
tablespoon oil in a saucepan, add rice and fry,
stirring, 2 to 3 minutes, until golden brown.
Stir in chile powder, raisins, almonds, thyme,
3/4 cup water and salt. Bring to a boil, then
reduce heat, cover and simmer 10 to 12 minutes, until rice has absorbed all the liquid.
Cool completely. Stuff chicken with rice.

Truss chicken neatly, then place in a steamer
and steam 1 hour. Heat remaining oil in a
large saucepan. Add cumin, turmeric, coriander, Garam Masala, salt and cayenne; cook 1
minute. Transfer chicken to this pan and
cook 5 minutes, turning chicken with two
wooden spoons until well coated in spice mixture. Pour hot water down side of pan, cover
and cook over low heat 15 to 20 minutes, until
chicken is tender. Serve hot, garnished with
thyme sprigs.

Makes 4 servings.

Duck with Honey & Lime

4 (8-oz.) duck quarters, skinned
2 tablespoons vegetable oil
1 onion, finely chopped
2 garlic cloves, crushed
1 (1-inch) piece fresh gingerroot, finely sliced
8 green cardamom pods, bruised
1 (3-inch) cinnamon stick
3 tablespoons honey
Juice of 2 limes
Twists of lime, to garnish

Rinse duck; pat dry with paper towels. Slash meaty parts two or three times.

Place duck in a shallow non-metal dish. Set aside. Heat oil in a skillet, add onion and cook, stirring, until soft. Stir in garlic, gingerroot, cardamom pods and cinnamon and cook 2 minutes more. Stir in honey and lime juice, then pour over duck. Cover and refrigerate 2 to 3 hours.

Preheat oven to 400F (205C). Transfer duck to a roasting pan. Roast 45 to 60 minutes, until browned and tender, basting occasionally with marinade. Serve hot, garnished with lime twists.

Makes 4 servings.

Moghul Shredded Duck

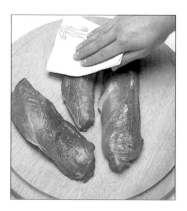

1 lb. boneless duck breasts, skinned
4 tablespoons vegetable oil
1 onion, finely chopped
1 recipe Nut Masala made with 3/4 cup cashew
  nuts, page 10
1 teaspoon ground turmeric
2/3 cup shredded coconut
1/2 cup raisins
2/3 cup plain yogurt
6 tablespoons whipping cream
1/3 cup unsalted cashew nuts
1 green chile, seeded, chopped

Rinse duck breasts; pat dry with paper towels.

Slice duck into 1/4-inch-thick strips. Heat 3 tablespoons oil in a large skillet, add duck and cook over high heat about 5 minutes, until browned all over. Remove duck from pan with a slotted spoon and set aside. Add onion to pan and cook, stirring, 5 minutes, or until soft. Stir in Nut Masala and turmeric; cook 2 minutes. Stir in coconut, raisins, yogurt, cream and duck.

Cover and cook over low heat 15 to 20 minutes, until duck is tender, stirring occasionally. Just before serving, heat remaining oil in a small pan, add cashew nuts and fry 2 to 3 minutes, until golden. Add chile and fry 1 minute more. Transfer duck to a warm serving dish, spoon over cashew nut and chile mixture. Serve hot.

Makes 4 to 6 servings.

Chicken with Lentils

8 oz. boneless chicken breasts
1-1/4 cups red split lentils
3 cups water
1/2 teaspoon ground turmeric
4 tablespoons vegetable oil
6 green cardamom pods, bruised
1 onion, finely sliced
1 (1/2-inch) piece fresh gingerroot, grated
Salt and red (cayenne) pepper to taste
2 tablespoons lemon juice
2/3 cup water
1 teaspoon cumin seeds
2 garlic cloves, finely sliced

Rinse chicken, pat dry with paper towels and cut into cubes. Set aside.

Wash lentils, place in a large saucepan and add 3 cups water and turmeric. Bring to a boil, then reduce heat, cover and simmer 20 to 30 minutes, or until tender. Drain thoroughly. Meanwhile, heat half the oil in a large saucepan, add cardamom pods and fry 1 minute. Add onion and fry, stirring frequently, about 8 minutes, until golden brown. Add chicken and fry 5 minutes, until browned all over. Add gingerroot and fry 1 minute more. Season with salt and cayenne.

Stir in lemon juice and 2/3 cup water. Cover and simmer 25 to 30 minutes, or until chicken is tender. Stir in lentil mixture and cook, stirring, 5 minutes more. Meanwhile, heat remaining oil in a small pan, add cumin seeds and garlic and fry, stirring, over medium heat 1 to 2 minutes, until garlic is golden. Transfer chicken and lentil mixture to a serving dish and pour garlic mixture over the top. Serve hot.

Makes 4 servings.

Chicken Tikka

1-1/2-lbs. boneless chicken breasts, skinned
2/3 cup plain yogurt
1 (1-inch) piece fresh gingerroot, grated
2 garlic cloves, crushed
1 teaspoon chile powder
1 tablespoon ground coriander
Salt to taste
2 tablespoons lime juice
2 tablespoons vegetable oil
Lime slices, to garnish

Rinse chicken, pat dry with paper towels and cut into 3/4-inch cubes. Thread onto short skewers.

Put skewered chicken into a shallow non-metal dish. In a small bowl, mix together yogurt, gingerroot, garlic, chile powder, coriander, salt, lime juice and oil. Pour over skewered chicken and turn to coat completely in marinade. Cover and refrigerate 6 hours or overnight to allow chicken to absorb flavors.

Heat grill. Place skewered chicken on grill rack and cook 5 to 7 minutes, turning skewers and basting occasionally with any remaining marinade. Serve hot, garnished with lime slices.

Makes 4 servings.

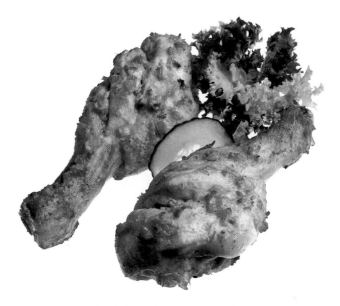

Fried Chicken Drumsticks

8 chicken drumsticks, skinned
1 onion, finely chopped
1 green chile, seeded, finely chopped
1 (1-inch) piece fresh gingerroot, grated
2/3 cup plain yogurt
1/4 teaspoon chile powder
Salt and pepper to taste
Vegetable oil for deep-frying
2 tablespoons chopped cilantro (fresh
    coriander)
Lettuce leaves and cucumber slices, to garnish

Rinse chicken drumsticks; pat dry with paper towels. Slash the meaty parts two or three times and place in a shallow non-metal dish.

Mix together onion, chile, gingerroot, yogurt, chile powder, salt and pepper. Pour over drumsticks and turn them in marinade until coated completely. Cover and refrigerate 2 to 3 hours to allow chicken to absorb flavors.

Half-fill a deep pan or deep-fryer with oil and heat to 375F (190C) or until a 1-inch bread cube browns in 50 seconds. Fry drumsticks four at a time 10 to 12 minutes, until browned, and cooked through. Drain on paper towels and keep warm, until all are cooked. Sprinkle with cilantro and serve hot, garnished with lettuce and cucumber.

Makes 4 servings.

Note: These chicken drumsticks are equally delicious served cold.

Chicken in Spicy Sauce

8 chicken thighs, skinned
1 (8-oz.) can tomatoes, drained
2 tablespoons tomato paste
2 tablespoons chile sauce
2 teaspoons sugar
1 tablespoon Garam Masala, page 11
2 tablespoons light soy sauce
1 (2-inch) piece fresh gingerroot, grated
2 garlic cloves, crushed
Juice of 1 lime and 1 lemon
Twists of lime peel and lemon peel, to garnish

Rinse chicken; pat dry with paper towels. Slash meaty parts of chicken two or three times.

Place chicken in a shallow non-metal dish and set aside. Put tomatoes, tomato paste, chile sauce, sugar, Garam Masala, soy sauce, gingerroot, garlic, lime juice and lemon juice in a blender or food processor fitted with the metal blade; process until pureed. Pour over chicken, cover and refrigerate 2 to 3 hours to allow chicken to absorb flavors.

Preheat oven to 375F (190C). Put chicken and the sauce in a roasting pan and cook, uncovered, 45 to 50 minutes, or until tender, basting with sauce two or three times during cooking. Serve hot, garnished with twists of lime and lemon.

Makes 4 servings.

Curried Chicken Livers

8 oz. chicken livers
2 tablespoons vegetable oil
2 onions, finely sliced
3 garlic cloves, crushed
2 teaspoons Garam Masala, page 11
1/2 teaspoon ground turmeric
Salt and pepper to taste
2 tablespoons lemon juice
2 tablespoons chopped fresh parsley
Parsley sprigs, to garnish

Rinse chicken livers and remove any green-tinged parts. Set aside.

Heat oil in a skillet, add onions and cook, stirring, over medium heat about 8 minutes, until soft and golden brown. Stir in garlic, Garam Masala, turmeric, salt and pepper. Cook 1 minute, then stir in chicken livers and fry about 5 minutes, stirring frequently, until livers are browned on outside, but still slightly pink in the center. Sprinkle with lemon juice and parsley. Serve hot, garnished with parsley sprigs.

Makes 4 appetizer servings.

Note: Frozen chicken livers can be used; thaw and drain before using.

Sweet Saffron Rice

1-1/2 cups basmati rice
1 teaspoon saffron threads
3 tablespoons boiling water
3 tablespoons vegetable oil
6 whole cloves
6 green cardamom pods, bruised
1 (3-inch) cinnamon stick
1/2 cup raisins
3 tablespoons sugar
Salt to taste
Flat-leaf parsley sprigs

Place rice in a sieve and rinse under cold running water until water runs clear.

Put rice in a bowl with 2-1/2 cups water and soak 30 minutes. Put saffron in a small bowl, add boiling water and soak. Heat oil in a heavy saucepan, add cloves, cardamom pods and cinnamon and cook 1 minute. Drain rice and reserve the soaking water. Add rice to the pan and cook 2 to 3 minutes until opaque and light golden.

Stir in reserved water, saffron and its soaking water, raisins, sugar and salt. Bring to a boil, then reduce heat and cover. Simmer 12 to 15 minutes, stirring once or twice until liquid is absorbed and rice is very tender. Remove spices before serving. Serve hot, garnished with parsley.

Makes 4 servings.

Note: The whole spices in the rice are not meant to be eaten.

Fragrant Fried Rice

1-1/4 cups basmati rice
3 tablespoons vegetable oil
8 whole cloves
4 black cardamom pods, bruised
1 bay leaf
1 (3-inch) cinnamon stick
1 teaspoon black peppercorns
1 teaspoon cumin seeds
1 teaspoon coriander seeds
Salt to taste
1 small cauliflower, cut into tiny flowerets
1 onion, sliced into rings
Onion rings and bay leaves, to garnish

Place rice in a sieve and rinse under cold running water until water runs clear.

Put in a bowl with 2-1/2 cups water and soak 30 minutes. Heat oil in a heavy saucepan, add cloves, cardamom pods, bay leaf, cinnamon, peppercorns, cumin seeds, coriander seeds and cook 1 minute. Add onion and cook 5 minutes, until softened. Drain rice and re-serve the soaking water.

Add rice to the pan and cook 2 to 3 minutes until opaque and light golden. Stir in reserved water, salt and cauliflower. Bring to a boil, reduce heat and cover. Simmer 12 to 15 minutes, stirring once or twice, until liquid is absorbed and rice and cauliflower are tender. Remove whole spices before serving. Serve hot, garnished with onion rings and bay leaves.

Makes 4 servings.

Note: The whole spices in the rice are not meant to be eaten.

Lentil-Stuffed Peppers

2/3 cup red split lentils
4 tablespoons vegetable oil
4 medium green or red bell peppers
1 teaspoon cumin seeds
2 onions, finely chopped
2 green chiles, seeded, chopped
1 (1-inch) piece fresh gingerroot, grated
1 tablespoon ground coriander
1-1/4 cups water
Salt and pepper to taste
2 tablespoons chopped cilantro (fresh
    coriander)
Cilantro leaves, to garnish

Rinse lentils, then soak in cold water 30 minutes.

Heat half the oil in a skillet. Add peppers and cook 3 to 5 minutes, until golden brown. Drain on paper towels; cool. Add remaining oil to pan, add cumin seeds; cook until just beginning to pop. Add onions and chiles and cook, stirring, 8 minutes, until onions are soft and golden brown. Stir in gingerroot and ground coriander. Drain lentils; add to pan with 1-1/4 cups water. Stir well, then cover.

Cook over low heat 15 to 20 minutes, until tender and liquid has evaporated. Stir in salt, pepper and cilantro. Preheat oven to 350F (175C). Cut tops from peppers and remove seeds. Stuff peppers with lentil mixture and replace tops. Stand in a baking dish. Bake 15 to 20 minutes until peppers are soft. Serve hot, garnished with cilantro leaves.

Makes 4 servings.

Stuffed Okra

1 lb. small okra
2 tablespoons mango powder, see note below
1 tablespoon ground coriander
2 teaspoons ground cumin
1/4 teaspoon red (cayenne) pepper
1 teaspoon Garam Masala, page 11
Salt to taste
2 tablespoons vegetable oil
1 onion, sliced
6 tomatoes, peeled
Lemon slices, to garnish

Rinse okra and pat dry with paper towel. Trim off stems, then cut a slit along one side of each pod stopping 1/4 inch from each end. Mix together mango powder, coriander, cumin, cayenne, Garam Masala and salt.

Pry open okra pods with your thumb and sprinkle a little of the spice mix inside each pod. Set aside.

Heat oil in a large saucepan and add onion. Cook about 5 minutes until softened. Cut tomatoes into wedges, remove and discard seeds. Add tomatoes to pan and cook, stirring once or twice, 2 minutes. Add okra, cover and cook gently 10 to 15 minutes, stirring occasionally until tender. Serve hot, garnished with lemon slices.

Makes 4 servings.

Note: Mango powder is available from Asian shops, where it is often called *amchoor* powder.

Dhal Balls with Yogurt

2/3 cup whole green lentils
1 cup plain yogurt
6 tablespoons chopped cilantro (fresh
    coriander)
1/4 teaspoon chile powder
4 tablespoons shredded fresh coconut
1 cup fresh bread crumbs
2 green chiles, seeded, chopped
1 (1-inch) piece fresh gingerroot, grated
1 egg, beaten
Salt and pepper to taste
1/2 cup whole-wheat flour
Vegetable oil for deep-frying
Cilantro (fresh coriander) leaves, to garnish

Put lentils in a sieve and rinse thoroughly under cold running water.

Pick over lentils and remove any grit. Put in a bowl, cover with cold water and soak 2 hours. Meanwhile, mix yogurt with 2 tablespoons of the cilantro and the chile powder. Cover and refrigerate. Drain lentils, cover with fresh water and simmer 30 minutes, or until tender. Puree in a vegetable mill or food processor, or mash well. Transfer to a bowl, add 2 tablespoons of the coconut, the bread crumbs, remaining cilantro, chiles, gingerroot, egg, salt and pepper; mix well. Refrigerate 30 minutes.

With damp hands, carefully roll mixture into 1-inch balls, then roll balls in flour to coat completely. Half-fill a deep pan or deep-fryer with oil and heat to 375F (190C), or until a 1-inch cube of bread browns in 50 seconds. Fry about 6 balls at a time 2 to 3 minutes, until golden brown. Drain on paper towels. Serve hot with yogurt sauce, sprinkled with remaining coconut and garnished with cilantro leaves.

Makes 4 servings.

Carrots with Fresh Dill

1 lb. carrots
1 tablespoon vegetable oil
2 tablespoons butter
3/4 teaspoon cumin seeds
Pinch ground asafetida
1 (1/2-inch) piece fresh gingerroot, finely
    chopped
2 green chiles, seeded, finely sliced
1 teaspoon ground coriander
1/4 teaspoon ground turmeric
6 tablespoons water
4 tablespoons chopped fresh dill
Salt to taste
Dill sprigs, to garnish

Cut carrots into 1/8- x 1-inch strips. Set aside.
Heat oil and butter in a heavy saucepan and
cook cumin seeds about 30 seconds, until they
begin to pop. Add asafetida, gingerroot,
chiles, coriander and turmeric; cook 2 minutes. Stir in carrots and water.

Cover and cook over medium heat 5 minutes,
or until carrots are just tender. Uncover, add
chopped dill and salt, increase heat and cook
over high heat about 2 minutes to evaporate
any excess liquid. Serve hot, garnished with
dill sprigs.

Makes 4 servings.

Note: This recipe is also delicious chilled and
served as a salad.

Mixed Vegetable Curry

3 tablespoons vegetable oil
1 onion, sliced
1 teaspoon ground cumin
1 teaspoon chile powder
2 teaspoons ground coriander
1 teaspoon ground turmeric
8 ounces potatoes, diced
6 ounces cauliflower, broken into flowerets
4 ounces green beans, sliced
6 ounces carrots, diced
4 tomatoes, peeled, chopped
1-1/4 cups hot vegetable stock
Onion rings, to garnish

Heat oil in a large saucepan, add onion and cook 5 minutes until softened. Stir in cumin, chile powder, coriander and turmeric; cook 2 minutes. Add potatoes, cauliflower, green beans and carrots, tossing them in the spices until coated.

Add tomatoes and stock and cover. Bring to a boil, then reduce heat and simmer 10 to 12 minutes or until vegetables are just tender. Serve hot, garnished with onion rings.

Makes 4 servings.

Variation: Use any mixture of vegetables to make a total of 1-1/2 pounds—turnips, zucchini, eggplant, parsnips and leeks are all suitable.

Spiced Brown Lentils

1-1/4 cups whole brown lentils
1-1/4 cups Coconut Milk, page 11
1/4 teaspoon chile powder
1/2 teaspoon ground turmeric
2 tablespoons vegetable oil
1 onion, finely chopped
4 curry leaves, optional
1/2 stalk lemon grass
1 (3-inch) cinnamon stick
Lemon thyme sprigs, to garnish

Rinse lentils, put in a bowl, cover with cold water and leave to soak 6 hours or overnight.

Drain lentils and put them in a large saucepan with Coconut Milk, chile powder and turmeric. Bring to a boil, cover and simmer 30 minutes, or until just tender. Heat oil in a separate pan, add onion, curry leaves, lemon grass and cinnamon and fry, stirring, over a medium heat 8 minutes, or until onion is soft and golden brown.

Stir into lentil mixture and simmer another 10 minutes, or until liquid has evaporated and lentils are soft but not broken up. Remove whole spices and serve hot, garnished with thyme sprigs.

Makes 4 servings.

Note: Substitute a few sprigs of lemon thyme if lemon grass is unavailable.

Curried Garbanzo Beans

1 cup dried garbanzo beans
Salt to taste
2 tablespoons vegetable oil
1 small onion, finely chopped
1 (1-inch) piece fresh gingerroot, grated
2 garlic cloves, crushed
1/2 teaspoon ground turmeric
1 teaspoon ground cumin
1 teaspoon Garam Masala, page 11
1/2 teaspoon chile powder
2 tablespoons chopped cilantro (fresh
   coriander)

Rinse garbanzo beans, put them in a bowl, cover with cold water and soak overnight.

Drain beans, add 2 cups cold water and salt. Boil 10 minutes, then reduce heat and simmer, partially covered 1 hour. In a separate pan, heat oil, add onion; cook about 8 minutes, until soft and golden brown.

Add gingerroot, garlic, turmeric, cumin, Garam Masala and chile powder; cook 1 minute. Stir in beans and their cooking water and bring to a boil. Cover and simmer 20 minutes, until beans are very tender, but still whole. Serve hot, sprinkled with chopped cilantro.

Makes 4 servings.

Mung Bean Sprout Salad

1 cup mung beans
2 green chiles, seeded, chopped
1 (1-inch) piece fresh gingerroot, grated
2/3 cup shredded fresh coconut
1/2 cucumber, diced
Juice of 1 lemon
Salt and pepper to taste
1 mango
2 tablespoons vegetable oil
1/2 teaspoon mustard seeds
Cilantro (fresh coriander) leaves and shredded
　　lemon peel, to garnish, if desired

Rinse beans, put in a bowl and cover with cold water.

Soak in warm water 30 minutes. Drain, then place in a sprouting tray and leave about two days, rinsing thoroughly every 12 hours, until beans germinate. Rinse well and drain. Place sprouts in a bowl and stir in chiles, gingerroot, coconut, cucumber, lemon juice and salt and pepper.

Peel and seed mango and dice flesh, stir into salad. Heat oil in a small pan. Add mustard seeds; cook 1 minute, until they begin to pop. Pour contents of pan over the salad and toss well to combine. Refrigerate at least 30 minutes, then serve, garnished with cilantro leaves and lemon peel.

Makes 4 to 6 servings.

Variation: Other beans, seeds and grains that sprout easily can be used for this salad—try whole-wheat kernels or alfalfa seeds.

Tamil Nadu Vegetables

2/3 cup red split lentils
1/2 teaspoon ground turmeric
2-1/2 cups water
1 small eggplant
1/4 cup vegetable oil
1/3 cup shredded coconut
1 teaspoon cumin seeds
1/2 teaspoon mustard seeds
2 dried red chiles, crushed
1 red bell pepper, seeded, sliced
4 ounces zucchini, thickly sliced
3 ounces green beans, cut into 3/4-inch pieces
2/3 cup vegetable stock
Salt to taste
Red bell pepper strips, to garnish

Rinse lentils and put in a large pan with turmeric and water. Boil 10 minutes, then reduce heat and cover.

Simmer 15 to 20 minutes until lentils are soft. Meanwhile, cut eggplant into 1/2-inch cubes. Heat oil in a large shallow pan, add coconut, cumin seeds, mustard seeds and chiles.

Cook 1 minute, then add eggplant, bell pepper, zucchini, green beans, stock and salt. Bring to a boil, reduce heat, cover and simmer 10 to 15 minutes, until vegetables are just tender. Stir in lentils and any cooking liquid and cook another 5 minutes. Serve hot, garnished with bell pepper strips.

Makes 4 servings.

Spinach & Bean Dumplings

1 cup yellow split mung beans
2 ounces frozen chopped spinach, thawed
2 tablespoons chopped cilantro (fresh
    coriander)
2 green chiles, seeded, chopped
Large pinch baking powder
1/2 teaspoon salt
Vegetable oil for deep-frying
Chile flowers, to garnish

Put beans in a bowl, cover them in water and soak 4 hours. Drain and rinse under cold running water.

Put beans in a blender or food processor fitted with the metal blade and process, until smooth, light and fluffy, scraping mixture from sides of bowl several times. Press excess water from spinach and mix into the ground beans. Stir in cilantro, chiles, baking powder and salt.

Half-fill a deep pan or deep-fryer with oil and heat to 375F (190C) or until a 1-inch bread cube browns in 50 seconds. Drop 6 level tablespoons of mixture into the hot oil; fry 4 to 5 minutes, or until golden brown. Drain dumplings on paper towel and keep warm while cooking remaining mixture. Serve hot, garnished with chile flowers.

Makes 4 servings.

Mushroom Curry

1 pound button mushrooms
2 green chiles, seeded
2 teaspoons ground coriander
1 teaspoon ground cumin
1/2 teaspoon chile powder
2 garlic cloves, crushed
1 onion, cut into wedges
2/3 cup Coconut Milk, page 11
Salt to taste
2 tablespoons butter
Fresh bay leaves, to garnish, if desired

Wipe mushrooms and trim stalks. Set aside.

Put chiles, coriander, cumin, chile powder, garlic, onion and Coconut Milk in a blender or food processor fitted with the metal blade and blend until smooth. Season to taste with salt.

Melt butter in a saucepan, add mushrooms and cook 3 to 4 minutes until golden brown. Add spice mixture, reduce heat and simmer, uncovered, 10 minutes, or until mushrooms are tender. Serve hot, garnished with bay leaves, if desired.

Makes 4 servings.

Peppers with Cauliflower

1/4 cup vegetable oil
1 large onion, sliced
2 garlic cloves, crushed
2 green chiles, seeded, chopped
1 cauliflower, cut into small flowerets
1/2 teaspoon ground turmeric
1 teaspoon Garam Masala, page 11
1/4 cup water
1 green bell pepper
1 red bell pepper
1 orange or yellow bell pepper
Salt and pepper to taste
1 tablespoon chopped cilantro (fresh
    coriander), to garnish

Heat oil in a large saucepan, add onion and cook over medium heat 8 minutes, or until soft and golden brown. Stir in garlic, chiles and cauliflowerets and cook 5 minutes, stirring occasionally. Stir in turmeric and Garam Masala; cook 1 minute.

Reduce heat and add water. Cover and cook 10 to 15 minutes, until cauliflower is almost tender. Meanwhile, cut peppers in half lengthwise, remove stalks and seeds and thinly slice peppers. Add to pan and cook another 3 to 5 minutes, until softened. Season with salt and pepper. Serve hot, garnished with chopped cilantro.

Makes 4 servings.

Cheesy Stuffed Tomatoes

8 tomatoes
2 tablespoons vegetable oil
1 small onion, finely chopped
1 garlic clove, crushed
1 (1-inch) piece fresh gingerroot, grated
1 teaspoon ground cumin
1/2 teaspoon ground turmeric
1/2 teaspoon red (cayenne) pepper
2 teaspoons ground coriander
Salt to taste
1/2 cup fresh farmers cheese
1/4 cup shredded Cheddar cheese
1 tablespoon chopped cilantro (fresh coriander)

Cut a slice from the top of each tomato. Scoop out centers, discard seeds, then chop pulp and reserve. Turn tomatoes upside down on paper towels and drain.

Heat oil in a small skillet, add onion and cook 5 minutes or until soft, stirring occasionally. Stir in garlic and gingerroot and cook 1 minute. Stir in cumin, turmeric, cayenne, coriander and salt; cook 1 minute more.

Stir in tomato pulp and cook, uncovered, about 5 minutes, until thick. Preheat oven to 375F (190C). Stir farmers cheese and half the Cheddar cheese into spice mixture and spoon into tomato shells. Sprinkle remaining Cheddar cheese on top and place in a baking pan. Bake 10 to 15 minutes, until tops are golden brown and tomatoes are soft. Sprinkle with chopped cilantro and serve hot.

Makes 4 servings.

Onion Bhajis

3/4 cup garbanzo bean flour, sifted
1 tablespoon vegetable oil plus extra for
    deep-frying
1 teaspoon ground coriander
1 teaspoon ground cumin
Salt to taste
2 green chiles, seeded, finely chopped
1/2 cup warm water
2 onions, finely sliced
Cilantro (fresh coriander) leaves, to garnish

Put flour in a blender or food processor fitted with the metal blade. Add 1 tablespoon oil, coriander, cumin, salt, chiles and water. Process until blended and smooth. Pour batter into a bowl, cover and let stand in a warm place 30 minutes.

Stir in onions. Half-fill a deep pan or deep-fryer with oil and heat over medium heat to 375F (190C) or until a 1-inch bread cube browns in 50 seconds. Add mixture in 2 tablespoon amounts to oil in batches; fry 5 to 6 minutes until golden. Do not cook too quickly or the centers will not cook completely. Drain on paper towels. Serve hot, garnished with cilantro leaves.

Makes 4 servings.

Spicy Okra

12 ounces okra
2 tablespoons vegetable oil
1 (1-inch) piece fresh gingerroot, grated
1 teaspoon ground turmeric
1/2 teaspoon chile powder
Salt to taste
1 teaspoon garbanzo bean flour
3 tablespoons water
1-1/4 cups plain yogurt
2 tablespoons chopped cilantro (fresh
    coriander), to garnish

Rinse okra and pat dry with paper towels, then cut into thick slices. Heat oil in a medium saucepan, add okra and cook 4 minutes, stirring occasionally. Stir in gingerroot, turmeric, chile powder, salt and flour; cook 1 minute more.

Stir in water, then cover and simmer 10 minutes, or until okra is tender. Stir in yogurt and reheat gently. Serve hot, sprinkled with cilantro.

Makes 4 servings.

Note: Choose okra pods that are about 4 inches long—larger pods are tough and stringy to eat.

Dry Potato Curry

1 pound red potatoes
Salt to taste
2 tablespoons vegetable oil
1 teaspoon mustard seeds
1 onion, finely sliced
2 garlic cloves
1 (1-inch) piece fresh gingerroot, grated
1 green chile, seeded, chopped
1 teaspoon ground turmeric
1/2 teaspoon red (cayenne) pepper
1 teaspoon ground cumin
Green bell pepper strips, to garnish, if desired

Cut potatoes into 3/4-inch chunks.

Cook potatoes in boiling salted water 6 to 8 minutes, until just tender. Drain and set aside. Heat oil in a large saucepan, add mustard seeds and cook 5 minutes, until soft, but not brown. Stir in garlic and gingerroot; cook 1 minute more.

Add cooked potatoes, chile, turmeric, cayenne and cumin and stir well. Cover and cook 3 to 5 minutes, stirring occasionally, until potatoes are very tender and coated with spices. Serve hot, garnished with bell pepper strips.

Makes 4 servings.

Fish in a Package

4 (6- to 8-oz.) fish steaks, such as sea bass, cod
  or salmon
1 or 2 fresh or frozen banana leaves, optional
Salt and pepper to taste
1-1/4 cups finely grated fresh coconut
2 ounces fresh mint, chopped
4 garlic cloves, crushed
1 teaspoon ground cumin
4 green chiles, seeded, chopped
2 tablespoons lemon juice
1/4 cup cider vinegar
1 tablespoon vegetable oil
3/4 cup water
8 dried curry leaves, optional
Mint leaves and lemon slices, to garnish

Wipe fish steaks and place each in center of a
12-inch square of banana leaf or foil. Sprinkle
fish with salt and pepper. Mix together coconut, mint, garlic, cumin, chiles and lemon
juice in a medium bowl. Spoon a quarter of
mixture on each fish steak. Fold sides of banana leaf or foil over to seal completely. Tie
banana leaf parcels with fine string, if necessary.

Pour vinegar, oil and water into the bottom of
a large steamer, add curry leaves and bring to
a boil. Place fish package over boiling liquid.
Steam 12 to 15 minutes, or until fish just
begins to flake. Open packages and serve,
garnished with mint and lemon slices.

Makes 4 servings.

Hot Mussels with Cumin

3 pounds mussels
2 tablespoons vegetable oil
1 large onion, finely chopped
1 (1-inch) piece fresh gingerroot, grated
6 garlic cloves, crushed
2 green chiles, seeded, finely chopped
1/2 teaspoon ground turmeric
2 teaspoons ground cumin
1 cup water
1-3/4 cups shredded fresh coconut
2 tablespoons chopped cilantro (fresh
    coriander)
Cilantro (fresh coriander) leaves, to garnish

Scrub mussels clean in several changes of fresh cold water and pull off beards.

Discard any mussels that are cracked or do not close tightly when tapped. Set other mussels aside. Heat oil in a large saucepan and add onion. Cook, stirring, 5 minutes until soft, then add gingerroot, garlic, chiles, turmeric and cumin. Cook 2 minutes, stirring constantly.

Add mussels, coconut and water; bring to a boil. Cover and cook over high heat, shaking pan frequently, about 5 minutes or until mussels have opened. Discard any that remain closed. Spoon mussels into a serving dish, pour cooking liquid over mussels and sprinkle with chopped cilantro. Garnish with cilantro leaves and serve at once.

Makes 4 servings.

Cilantro & Chile Fish

1-3/4 lbs. white fish fillets, such as monkfish or
    sole
1 tablespoon plus 1 teaspoon lemon juice
Salt and pepper to taste
3 ounces cilantro (fresh coriander) leaves
4 green chiles, seeded, chopped
3 garlic cloves, crushed
1 to 2 tablespoons water
1 cup plain yogurt
Vegetable oil for deep-frying
Lemon wedges and cilantro (fresh coriander)
    leaves, to garnish

Trim any skin and bones from fish. Cut flesh
into 1- x 3-inch strips.

Spread fish strips in a shallow non-metal dish
and sprinkle with lemon juice, salt and pepper. Set aside. Put cilantro, chiles, garlic and
water in a blender or food processor fitted
with the metal blade and process, until
smooth, frequently scraping down mixture.
Squeeze out excess liquid from paste, place in
a shallow dish and stir in yogurt.

Heat oil in a deep pan or deep-fryer to 350F
(175C) or until a 1-inch bread cube browns in
65 seconds. Drain fish and pat dry with paper
towels. Dip the strips in yogurt mixture, coat-
ing them all over and fry a few at a time 2 to 3
minutes, until golden brown. Drain on paper
towels, then serve at once, garnished with
lemon wedges and cilantro leaves.

Makes 4 servings.

Sole with Dill Stuffing

4 (6-oz.) sole fillets, skinned
1 tablespoon lemon juice
Salt and pepper to taste
1-1/2 tablespoons vegetable oil
1 garlic clove, crushed
1 (1-inch) piece fresh gingerroot, grated
1/4 teaspoon red (cayenne) pepper
1/4 teaspoon ground turmeric
4 green onions, finely chopped
8 tablespoons finely chopped fresh dill
1/4 cup water
Dill sprigs, to garnish

Rinse fish fillets and pat dry with paper towels.

Lay fillets skinned side up on a work surface and sprinkle with lemon juice, salt and pepper. Set aside. Preheat oven to 350F (175C). Heat oil in a skillet. Add garlic, gingerroot, cayenne, turmeric and green onions. Cook over low heat 3 minutes or until onions are soft and golden, stirring occasionally. Remove from heat, cool, then stir in chopped dill.

Divide stuffing among fillets and spread evenly over fish. Roll fillets up from thickest end. Grease a shallow ovenproof dish. Arrange fish rolls, seam side down in the dish; add water. Cover with foil and bake 15 to 20 minutes, or until fish just begins to flake. Serve hot, topped with cooking juices and garnished with dill sprigs.

Makes 4 servings.

Spicy Garlic Fish Fry

1-1/2 lbs. mixed white fish fillets, such as sole, whiting, cod or monkfish
1 teaspoon ground cumin
1/2 teaspoon ground coriander
1 teaspoon ground anise seeds
1/2 teaspoon chile powder
3 garlic cloves, crushed
1 tablespoon lemon juice
Salt to taste
Vegetable oil for deep-frying
Lettuce leaves and sliced radishes, to garnish

Remove any skin and bones from fish, rinse and pat dry with paper towels. Cut into large chunks.

Mix together cumin, coriander, ground anise, chile powder, garlic, lemon juice and salt, blending to a smooth paste. Spread over fish, cover and refrigerate 1 hour.

Half-fill a deep pan or deep-fryer with oil and heat to 350F (175C) or until a 1-inch bread cube browns in 50 seconds. Cook fish, a few pieces at a time, 2 to 3 minutes, until golden brown. Drain on paper towels. Serve hot, garnished with lettuce and radish slices.

Makes 4 servings.

Spicy Shrimp Patties

12 ounces white fish fillets, such as sole, cod or
  whiting
6 ounces cooked peeled shrimp, chopped
4 green onions, chopped
1 (1-inch) piece fresh gingerroot, grated
2 tablespoons chopped cilantro (fresh
  coriander)
1 tablespoon chopped fresh mint
2 cups fresh white bread crumbs
Salt and red (cayenne) pepper to taste
1 egg yolk, beaten
2 tablespoons lemon juice
3/4 cup garbanzo bean flour
1 tablespoon ground coriander
1/2 cup water
1/4 cup vegetable oil
Mint sprigs and lemon slices, to garnish

Remove any skin and bones from fish, rinse
and pat dry with paper towels. Mince fish,
then transfer to a bowl. Stir in shrimp, green
onions, gingerroot, cilantro, mint, 1/2 cup of
bread crumbs, salt and cayenne. Add egg yolk
and lemon juice; mix well. Divide mixture
into 16 equal portions and form into 1/2-inch-
thick rounds. Roll patties in remaining bread
crumbs to coat completely.

Put flour, coriander, salt and cayenne in a
small bowl, add water and mix to a smooth
batter. Heat oil in a skillet. Dip patties in batter; fry 2 to 3 minutes on each side until
golden brown. Drain on paper towels and
serve hot, garnished with mint and lemon
slices.

Makes 4 servings.

Fish in Hot Sauce

4 (8-oz. each) whole fish, such as mackerel or
    trout, cleaned
4 dill sprigs
4 lime slices
4 tablespoons vegetable oil
4 green onions, sliced
1 (1/2-inch) piece fresh gingerroot, grated
1 garlic clove, crushed
1 teaspoon mustard seeds
1/4 teaspoon red (cayenne) pepper
1 tablespoon tamarind paste
2 tablespoons tomato paste
6 tablespoons water
Dill sprigs and lime slices, to garnish

Rinse fish and pat dry with paper towels.
Slash two or three times on each side with a
sharp knife and tuck a sprig of dill and a lime
slice inside each fish. Set aside. Heat 2 tablespoons of the oil in a small saucepan. Add
onions and cook, stirring, 2 to 3 minutes, until
softened. Add gingerroot, garlic and mustard
seeds; cook 1 minute more.

Stir in cayenne, tamarind paste, tomato paste
and water. Bring to a boil, reduce heat and
simmer, uncovered, about 5 minutes, until
thickened slightly. Meanwhile, heat grill.
Place fish on grill rack, brush with remaining
oil and cook about 5 minutes on each side,
until fish just begins to flake, basting occasionally with oil. Serve hot with the sauce.
Garnish with dill and lime slices.

Makes 4 servings.

Steamed Fish & Vegetables

4 (8-oz. each) whole red mullet, red snapper or
   sea bream, cleaned
1 tablespoon plus 1 teaspoon Garam Masala,
   page 11
1/2 teaspoon ground turmeric
2 tablespoons chopped cilantro (fresh
   coriander)
1 tablespoon chopped fresh parsley
1 (1-inch) piece fresh gingerroot, grated
4 lemon slices
2 tablespoons vegetable oil
8 new potatoes, sliced
3 carrots, sliced
4 zucchini, sliced
Salt and pepper to taste
Parsley sprigs, to garnish

Rinse fish and pat dry with paper towels.
Slash three times on each side. Mix together
Garam Masala, turmeric, cilantro, parsley
and gingerroot. Rub into flesh and skin of
fish. Tuck a slice of lemon inside each fish and
set aside. Heat oil in a skillet, add potatoes and
carrots and cook, stirring frequently, 5 to 6
minutes, until slightly softened and beginning to brown.

Add zucchini to pan and cook 1 minute more.
Season with salt and pepper. Using a slotted
spoon, transfer vegetables to a steamer. Lay
fish on top. Cover and steam 20 to 25 minutes, or until fish just starts to flake and vegetables are tender. Serve at once, garnished
with parsley.

Makes 4 servings.

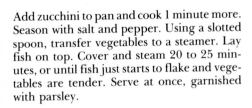

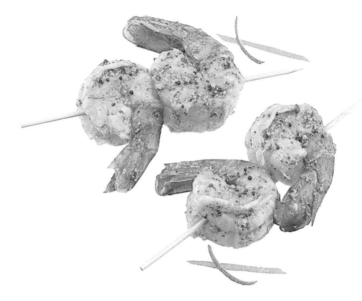

Shrimp & Mustard Seeds

1 pound large unpeeled shrimp
1 tablespoon mixed black and yellow mustard
   seeds
1/2 teaspoon ground turmeric
1/2 teaspoon red (cayenne) pepper
Salt to taste
6 tablespoons water
1 green chile, finely chopped
2 tablespoons butter, melted
Orange and lime peel, to garnish

Peel shrimp, leaving tail shells on. Make a small incision along the spines and remove black vein. Put two or three shrimp on each short wooden skewer. Set aside.

Reserve 1 teaspoon of mustard seeds. Grind remainder in a coffee grinder or with a mortar and pestle. Transfer to a medium bowl and mix in turmeric, cayenne and salt. Add water and chile; blend to a smooth paste. Add shrimp, turning to coat them in the paste; refrigerate 30 minutes.

Preheat boiler. Place skewers on a broiler rack, brush with butter and sprinkle with reserved mustard seeds. Cook 3 to 5 minutes, until shrimp are pink, turning over once and basting occasionally with any remaining marinade. Serve hot, garnished with orange and lime peel.

Makes 4 servings.

Madras Curried Crab

4 cooked medium crab
3 tablespoons vegetable oil
1 onion, finely chopped
3 garlic cloves, finely sliced
1 (1-inch) piece fresh gingerroot, grated
1 large tomato, peeled, chopped
3 green chiles, seeded, chopped
2 tablespoons shredded coconut, toasted
1 recipe Nut Masala, made with almonds, page 10
1 cup Coconut Milk, page 11

Remove large claws from crabs and crack to make eating easier. Twist off small claws.

Remove the top or back shells, remove finger-shaped gills and discard. Cut bottom shell in half with a large sharp knife or cleaver and use a skewer to remove all the white meat. Remove and discard the small sack at top of crab shells and any green-colored matter. Scrape out creamy brown meat from shells and add to white meat. Rinse shells thoroughly and set aside.

Heat oil in a large skillet, add onion and cook, stirring frequently, about 8 minutes, or until soft and golden. Add garlic and gingerroot; cook 1 minute. Stir in tomato, chiles, coconut, masala, Coconut Milk and reserved crabmeat. Add crab claws, cover and simmer 6 to 8 minutes, until heated through. Spoon into crab shells and serve hot.

Makes 4 servings.

Shrimp & Fish Ball Curry

1 pound white fish fillets, such as sole, cod,
   whiting or monkfish, skinned
4 ounces cooked peeled shrimp
1-1/2 cups fresh white bread crumbs
2 eggs, beaten separately
2 tablespoons chopped cilantro (fresh
   coriander)
2 teaspoons lemon juice
Salt and pepper to taste
2 tablespoons vegetable oil plus extra for
   deep-frying
1 large onion, finely chopped
2 green chiles, seeded, chopped
4 garlic cloves, crushed
1/2 teaspoon ground turmeric
2/3 cup Coconut Milk, page 11
1 (14-oz.) can chopped tomatoes

Rinse fish and remove any bones. Mince fish
and shrimp, then transfer to a large bowl. Stir
in 1 cup of bread crumbs, 1 egg, cilantro,
lemon juice, salt and pepper. Mix well and
form into 24 balls. Roll balls in remaining egg,
then in remaining bread crumbs to coat completely. Cover and refrigerate 30 minutes.
Meanwhile, heat 2 tablespoons oil in a heavy
saucepan, add onion and cook, stirring, 5
minutes to soften.

Add chiles, garlic and turmeric; cook 2 minutes more. Stir in Coconut Milk and tomatoes
and cook, uncovered 20 minutes, until reduced and thickened, stirring occasionally.
Half-fill a deep pan or deep-fryer with oil and
heat to 375F (190C), or until a 1-inch bread
cube browns in 50 seconds. Fry fish balls 3 to 5
minutes, until golden brown. Drain on paper
towels and serve with the sauce.

Makes 4 servings.

Creamy Saffron Fish Curry

1-1/2 pounds white fish fillets, such as sole,
    whiting or cod
Pinch of saffron threads
2 tablespoons boiling water
3 tablespoons vegetable oil
2 onions, chopped
3 garlic cloves, crushed
1 (1-inch) piece fresh gingerroot, grated
1 teaspoon ground turmeric
1 tablespoon ground coriander
2 teaspoons Garam Masala, page 11
Salt and red (cayenne) pepper to taste
2 teaspoons garbanzo bean flour
1 cup plain yogurt
1/4 cup whipping cream
Shreds of lemon peel and red bell pepper, to
    garnish

Rinse fish, remove any skin and bones and pat
dry with paper towels. Cut into large chunks
and set aside. Put saffron in a small bowl with
boiling water; let soak. Heat oil in a large
shallow pan, add onions and cook, stirring,
about 5 minutes, until soft, but not brown.

Add garlic, gingerroot, turmeric, coriander,
Garam Masala, salt and cayenne; cook 1 minute more. Stir in flour; cook 1 minute, then
remove from heat. Stir in yogurt and cream;
bring slowly to a boil. Add fish. Reduce heat,
cover and simmer gently 10 to 15 minutes,
until fish just begins to flake. Serve hot, garnished with lemon peel and bell pepper.

Makes 4 servings.

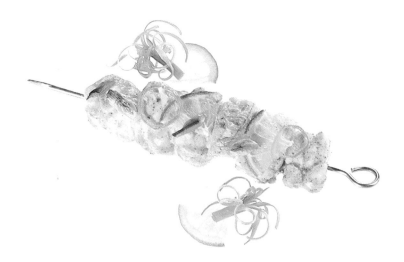

Coriander Fish Kabobs

1-1/2 pounds monkfish fillet
2/3 cup plain yogurt
3 garlic cloves, crushed
2 teaspoons Garam Masala, page 11
1 tablespoon ground coriander
Salt and pepper to taste
1 green chile, seeded, cut into thin rings
1 green onion, finely sliced
1 lime, quartered, finely sliced

Remove any bones from fish, rinse and pat dry with paper towels. Cut into 1-inch cubes and thread onto skewers.

Mix together yogurt, garlic, Garam Masala, coriander, salt and pepper. Put kabobs in a non-metal dish; add yogurt marinade. Cover and refrigerate 2 to 3 hours to allow fish to absorb flavors.

Preheat broiler. Place kabobs on a broiler rack; cook 3 to 4 minutes. Turn kabobs over, scatter chile, onion and lime slices over top; baste with any remaining marinade. Broil another 3 to 4 minutes, until fish just begins to flake. Serve hot.

Makes 4 servings.

Note: You can use other white fish fillets, such as sole instead of monkfish.

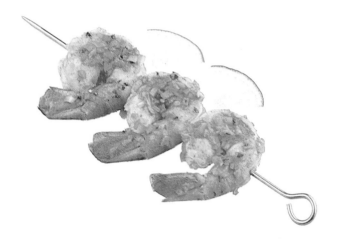

Prawn Kabobs

12 raw large shrimp
2 tablespoons vegetable oil
2 tablespoons lime juice
2 garlic cloves, crushed
1/2 teaspoon paprika
1/2 teaspoon ground turmeric
2 green chiles, seeded, finely chopped
1 tablespoon chopped cilantro (fresh coriander)
Lime slices, to garnish

Peel shrimp, leaving tail shells on. Make a small incision along the spines and remove black vein. Thread onto skewers and set aside.

Whisk together vegetable oil, lime juice, garlic, paprika and turmeric. Stir in chiles. Put skewered shrimp in a non-metal dish; add marinade. Cover and refrigerate 30 minutes, basting occasionally.

Preheat broiler. Drain skewered shrimp and place on a broiler rack. Cook 3 to 5 minutes, turning and basting occasionally with the marinade, until shrimp are pink. Sprinkle with cilantro and serve hot, garnished with lime slices.

Makes 4 servings.

Coconut Spiced Cod

4 (6- to 8-oz.) cod steaks
Salt and pepper to taste
2 tablespoons vegetable oil
1 onion, chopped
1-1/3 cups shredded coconut
1 (2-inch) piece fresh gingerroot, grated
2 garlic cloves, crushed
2 green chiles, seeded, chopped
1/2 teaspoon chile powder
Grated peel and juice of 1 lemon
2 tablespoons chopped cilantro (fresh
     coriander)
2 tomatoes, peeled, seeded and diced
Oregano sprigs, to garnish

Rinse cod steaks; pat dry with paper towels. Place in a greased baking dish; sprinkle with salt and pepper. Heat oil in a skillet, add onion and cook, stirring, about 5 minutes, or until soft. Stir in coconut, gingerroot, garlic, chiles and chile powder; cook, stirring, 3 to 5 minutes, until golden brown.

Stir in lemon peel and juice, cover and simmer 10 minutes to soften coconut. Preheat oven to 325F (160C). Stir cilantro and tomatoes into coconut mixture and spoon over steaks. Bake 20 to 25 minutes, until fish just begins to flake. Serve hot, garnished with oregano.

Makes 4 servings.

Note: Cover fish with foil during cooking if coconut begins to brown too much.

Grilled Spiced Fish

4 (8-oz.) sole, skinned
Salt and pepper to taste
2/3 cup plain yogurt
2 garlic cloves, crushed
2 teaspoons Garam Masala, page 11
1 teaspoon ground coriander
1/2 teaspoon chile powder
1 tablespoon lemon juice
Lemon wedges, to garnish

Rinse fish, pat dry with paper towels and place in a shallow non-metal dish. Sprinkle with salt and pepper.

Mix together yogurt, garlic, Garam Masala, coriander, chile powder and lemon juice. Pour over fish. Cover and refrigerate 2 to 3 hours to allow fish to absorb flavors.

Preheat broiler. Transfer fish to a broiler rack; cook about 8 minutes, until fish just begins to flake, basting with cooking juices and turning over halfway through cooking. Serve hot, garnished with lemon wedges.

Makes 4 servings.

Carrot Halva

1-1/4 lbs. carrots, coarsely grated
3 cups milk
8 green cardamom pods, bruised
1/4 cup vegetable oil
1/4 cup superfine sugar
2 tablespoons raisins
1/3 cup shelled pistachios, coarsely chopped
1 cup thick plain yogurt, to serve

Put carrots, milk and cardamom pods in a heavy saucepan; bring to a boil over high heat.

Reduce heat to medium and cook, uncovered, about 50 minutes, until liquid has been absorbed, stirring occasionally. Remove cardamom pods. Heat oil in a large skillet, add carrot mixture and cook, stirring constantly, 10 to 15 minutes, until mixture turns a deep red color.

Stir in sugar, raisins and half the pistachios. Cook 1 to 2 minutes more to heat through. Serve warm, topped with yogurt and sprinkled with remaining pistachios.

Makes 6 to 8 servings.

Pistachio Halva

1-1/4 cups shelled pistachios
1 cup boiling water
2 tablespoons milk
1/2 cup sugar
1-1/2 tablespoons butter or ghee
1 teaspoon vanilla extract

Put pistachios in a bowl, top with boiling water and soak 30 minutes. Grease and line an 8-inch square pan with waxed paper.

Drain pistachios thoroughly and put in a blender or food processor fitted with the metal blade. Add milk and process until finely chopped, scraping mixture down from sides once or twice. Stir in sugar. Heat a large nonstick skillet, add butter and melt over medium-low heat. Add nut paste and cook about 15 minutes, stirring constantly, until mixture is very thick.

Stir in vanilla extract, then spoon into prepared pan and spread evenly. Cool completely, then cut into 20 squares using a sharp knife.

Makes about 20 squares.

Note: This halva will keep 2 to 3 weeks, covered and stored in the refrigerator.

Fritters & Fragrant Syrup

2 cups sugar
2 cups water
5 green cardamom pods, bruised
1 teaspoon rose water
Pinch of saffron threads
1 cup all-purpose flour
1 tablespoon baking powder
2-1/3 cups nonfat dry milk powder
1 tablespoon butter, melted
2/3 cup plain yogurt
About 1/2 cup milk
1/3 cup raisins
Vegetable oil for frying
Rose petals, to decorate

Put sugar and water in a heavy saucepan and heat gently, stirring occasionally, until sugar dissolves. Increase heat and bring to a boil and boil for about 5 minutes, or until thickened and syrupy. Stir in rose water and saffron threads and keep warm. Meanwhile, sift together flour and baking powder into a medium bowl; stir in milk powder. Mix in butter and yogurt and enough milk to make a soft dough.

With floured hands, divide dough into 24 pieces. Make a depression in center of each and press in two or three raisins. Cover raisins with dough and roll into balls. Half-fill a deep pan or deep-fryer with oil and heat to 375F (190C) or until a 1-inch cube of bread browns in 50 seconds. Fry balls four or five at a time, 3 to 5 minutes until a deep golden brown. Drain on paper towels, then add to the syrup. Serve hot, decorated with rose petals.

Makes 24 fritters.

Cardamom & Nut Ice Cream

8 cups milk
12 green cardamom pods, bruised
1/3 cup sugar
1/3 cup chopped blanched almonds, toasted
1/3 cup chopped pistachios
Mint sprigs, to decorate

Put milk and cardamom pods in a large heavy saucepan and bring to a boil. Reduce heat to medium-low and simmer, uncovered, 30 minutes, or until milk is reduced by about two-thirds, stirring frequently. Remove cardamom pods with a slotted spoon and discard.

Stir in sugar, almonds and half the pistachios and simmer 5 minutes more. Cool. Pour reduced milk into a plastic container, cover and freeze 2 to 3 hours until frozen around edge. Spoon into a food processor fitted with the metal blade and process until smooth and light. Return to plastic container, cover and freeze 1 hour. Meanwhile, put 6 individual molds into freezer to chill.

Spoon semi-frozen mixture into molds, pressing down firmly. Cover and freeze for 2 to 3 hours until solid. Dip in hot water for a few seconds and turn out onto plates. Serve at once, sprinkled with remaining pistachios and decorated with mint.

Makes 6 servings.

Note: If preferred, beat ice cream with an electric mixer instead of a food processor.

Saffron Yogurt

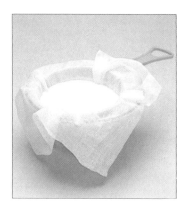

2-1/2 cups plain yogurt
Pinch of saffron threads
2 tablespoons boiling water
Seeds from 6 cardamom pods
3 tablespoons superfine sugar
Lemon peel and cardamom seeds, to decorate

Pour yogurt into a nylon sieve lined with cheesecloth and refrigerate to drain overnight.

Put saffron and boiling water in a small bowl and soak 30 minutes. Turn drained yogurt into a bowl and stir in saffron and its soaking liquid.

Put cardamom seeds in a mortar and crush lightly with a pestle. Stir into yogurt with sugar. Serve chilled, decorated with lemon peel and cardamom seeds.

Makes 4 to 6 servings.

Rose Water Pudding

1 (1/4-oz.) envelope (1 tablespoon) powdered
    gelatin
3 tablespoons water
2-1/2 cups milk
3 tablespoons sugar
2 teaspoons rose water
Few drops red food coloring
Pink rose petals, to decorate

Sprinkle gelatin over water in a small bowl and soften 2 to 3 minutes. Put milk in a separate saucepan and heat until almost boiling, add gelatin and stir until dissolved completely. Stir in sugar and rose water.

Pour half the mixture into a bowl, add a few drops red food coloring to color it a delicate pink and whisk until cool and frothy. Wet four 3/4-cup molds and divide pink mixture among them. Refrigerate about 30 minutes until mixture is just set, but still sticky on top. Meanwhile, keep remaining white mixture in a warm place to prevent it from setting. Whisk white mixture until frothy and pour into molds on top of set pink mixture.

Chill until set completely, then dip molds in hot water 1 to 2 seconds and turn out onto plates. Serve cold, decorated with rose petals.

Makes 4 servings.

Note: Before turning puddings out, wet each serving plate with a very little cold water to prevent them from sticking to the plate, allowing you to center them, if necessary.

Saffron Rice Pudding

1-1/4 cups basmati rice
2-1/2 cups water
1/3 cup milk
Pinch of saffron threads
2 tablespoons butter
2 green cardamom pods, bruised
1 (1-inch) cinnamon stick
2 cloves
1/2 cup raisins
1/4 cup sugar
1/3 cup sliced almonds, toasted

Wash rice under cold running water and put into a large saucepan with water.

Bring to a boil, reduce heat and simmer 5 minutes, then drain. Measure 2 tablespoons of milk into a small bowl, add saffron and soak 5 minutes. Heat butter in a heavy saucepan, add rice, cardamom pods, cinnamon and cloves and cook 2 to 3 minutes, or until rice becomes opaque.

Stir in remaining milk, saffron milk, raisins and sugar and bring to a boil. Cover and simmer about 6 to 8 minutes, until rice is tender and liquid has been absorbed. Remove whole spices and serve hot, with almonds scattered on top.

Makes 4 servings.

Coconut Pancakes

1 cup all-purpose flour
Pinch of salt
1 egg, beaten
1-1/4 cups milk
3 tablespoons brown sugar
3 cups shredded fresh coconut
1 (1/2-inch) piece fresh gingerroot, grated
6 anise seeds, crushed
Plain yogurt, to serve
1/3 cup shredded fresh coconut, to serve

Sift together flour and salt into a medium bowl. Whisk in egg and half of the milk to make a smooth, thick batter.

Set batter aside in a cool place 30 minutes, then stir in enough of remaining milk to make batter the consistency of light cream. Heat a 6-inch skillet over medium-high heat, brush with a little oil and pour in 2 to 3 tablespoons batter, tipping pan to coat bottom. Cook 1 to 2 minutes until browned, then flip pancake over and cook other side for about 30 seconds, until browned.

Turn pancake onto a plate and make about 7 more pancakes in same way, stacking them on the plate as they are ready. In a small bowl, mix together sugar, coconut, gingerroot and anise seeds. Spread a spoonful of mixture on each pancake and fold into quarters. Cover and refrigerate about 30 minutes. Serve cold with yogurt and coconut.

Makes 4 servings.

Golden Semolina Pudding

1/2 cup sugar
2/3 cup water
3 tablespoons butter or ghee
3/4 cup semolina
Seeds from 3 cardamom pods
1/4 cup raisins
1/2 cup sliced almonds, toasted

Put sugar and water in a heavy saucepan. Cook over low heat, stirring occasionally, until sugar has dissolved. Increase heat and bring to a boil and boil 1 minute. Remove from heat and set aside.

Melt butter in a large heavy skillet, add semolina and cook 8 to 10 minutes over medium heat, stirring constantly, until semolina turns golden brown.

Remove from heat and cool slightly, then stir in sugar syrup and cardamom seeds. Cook over low heat 3 to 5 minutes until thick, stirring frequently. Stir in half the raisins and almonds. Serve warm, decorated with remaining raisins and almonds.

Makes 4 to 6 servings.

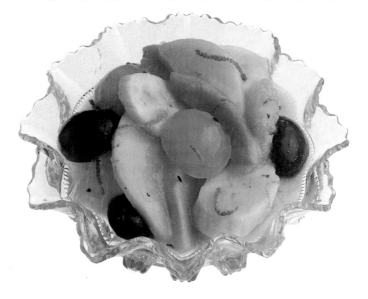

Indian Fruit Salad

2 mangoes
2 bananas
2 oranges
2 ounces black grapes
2 ounces green grapes
1 papaya
Grated peel and juice of 1 lime
1/4 cup superfine sugar
Freshly ground black pepper to taste
Plain yogurt, to serve

Peel and seed mangoes and cut flesh into thin slices, reserving any scraps. Peel and diagonally slice bananas.

Peel and section oranges, working over a bowl to catch juice. Halve and seed both black and green grapes. Peel and halve papaya, scoop out seeds and cut flesh into slices, reserving any scraps. Put fruit in a serving bowl and stir to combine. Put orange juice, lime juice, sugar and scraps of mango and papaya in blender or food processor fitted with the metal blade and process until smooth. Add lime peel and pepper. Pour over fruit and chill at least 1 hour before serving with yogurt.

Makes 4 to 6 servings.

Note: Substitute other fruits, such as melon, guava or pineapple, if preferred.

Toasted Almond Toffee

2 cups sugar
1 cup water
2 cups nonfat dry milk powder
1 teaspoon vanilla extract
1/4 cup flaked almonds, toasted

Grease and line an 8-inch square pan with waxed paper. Put sugar and water in a large heavy saucepan. Heat gently, stirring occasionally, until sugar is dissolved.

Increase heat and bring to a boil, and boil over medium-high heat until a few drops of mixture will form a soft ball in cold water. Stir in milk powder and cook 3 to 4 minutes more, stirring all the time, until mixture begins to dry on spoon. Stir in vanilla.

Pour into prepared pan and spread evenly. Scatter almonds over top and press into surface. Leave to cool slightly, then cut into 25 squares with a sharp knife while still warm. Leave in pan until cold and firm.

Makes 25 squares.

Coconut Layer Cake

1/2 cup all-purpose flour
1-2/3 cups Coconut Milk, page 11
6 egg yolks, beaten
1/2 cup sugar
Seeds from 4 green cardamom pods, crushed
Pinch of freshly grated nutmeg
1/2 cup butter, melted
Plain yogurt and sliced bananas, to serve

Put flour in a medium bowl, whisk in coconut milk, egg yolks, sugar, cardamom seeds and nutmeg, then let batter stand 30 minutes.

Preheat oven to 425F (220C). Butter a 6-inch soufflé dish. Add 1 tablespoon butter to dish and heat in oven 5 minutes. Pour in 6 tablespoons of batter and bake 10 to 15 minutes, until firm to the touch and lightly browned. Brush with butter. Continue adding another three layers, brushing each cooked layer with butter before adding batter. Bake each layer 10 to 15 minutes.

Put soufflé dish in a baking pan half-filled with boiling water, then continue adding another three layers in same way as before. When last layer is cooked, remove dish from oven and cool. Run a knife around edge of dish to loosen cake and turn out onto a serving plate. Serve warm, with yogurt and sliced bananas.

Makes 4 to 6 servings.

Apricot Dessert

1-3/4 cups dried apricots
1 cup water
1 cup superfine sugar
2 cups water
1/2 pint (1 cup) whipping cream
1/3 cup blanched almonds, chopped, toasted

Put apricots and 1 cup water in a medium saucepan; bring to a boil. Reduce heat, cover and simmer about 25 minutes, or until very soft.

Meanwhile, put sugar and 2 cups water in a heavy saucepan and heat gently, stirring occasionally, until sugar has dissolved. Increase heat, bring to a boil and boil 3 minutes, or until syrupy. Drain apricots and puree in a blender or food processor fitted with the metal blade. Add syrup and process again.

Pour into a bowl and cool, then refrigerate at least 1 hour. Whip cream until soft peaks form, fold half into apricot puree, leaving it slightly marbled, and spoon into serving dishes. Chill 30 minutes, then top with remaining cream and scatter with chopped almonds.

Makes 4 to 6 servings.

Cashew Nut Fudge

1-1/2 cups unsalted cashew nuts
1-1/2 cups boiling water
2 tablespoons milk
2/3 cup sugar
1 tablespoon butter or ghee
1 teaspoon vanilla extract
Few sheets of silver leaf, page 17

Put cashew nuts in a bowl, top with boiling water and soak 1 hour. Grease and line an 8-inch square pan with waxed paper.

Drain cashew nuts thoroughly and put in a blender or food processor fitted with the metal blade. Add milk and process until smooth, scraping mixture down from side once or twice. Stir in sugar. Heat a large non-stick skillet, add butter and melt over medium-low heat. Add nut paste and cook about 20 minutes, stirring constantly, until mixture is very thick.

Stir in vanilla extract, then spoon into prepared pan and spread evenly. Cool completely, then press silver leaf onto surface. Cut fudge into about 25 diamond shapes using a wet sharp knife.

Makes about 25 pieces.

Note: This fudge will keep for two to three weeks if stored in an airtight container.

Fresh Mango Chutney

2 mangoes
1 red chile, seeded, finely sliced
1/4 cup chopped cashew nuts
1/4 cup raisins
2 tablespoons chopped fresh mint
Pinch of asafetida
1/2 teaspoon ground cumin
1/4 teaspoon red (cayenne) pepper
1/2 teaspoon ground coriander
Mint sprigs, to garnish

Peel and seed mangoes, then very thinly slice flesh.

Put mango slices in a bowl with chile, cashew nuts, raisins and chopped mint; stir gently. In a small bowl, mix together asafetida, cumin, cayenne and coriander; sprinkle over mango mixture.

Stir gently to coat mango mixture in spices, then cover and refrigerate 2 hours. Serve cold, garnished with mint sprigs.

Makes about 2 cups.

Lime Pickle

12 limes
1/4 cup coarse sea salt
1 tablespoon fenugreek seeds
1 tablespoon mustard seeds
2 tablespoons chile powder
1 tablespoon ground turmeric
1 cup vegetable oil
Cilantro (fresh coriander) leaves, to garnish

Cut each lime lengthways into 8 thin wedges. Place in a large sterilized bowl, sprinkle with salt and set aside.

Put fenugreek and mustard seeds in a skillet and dry roast them over medium heat 1 to 2 minutes, until they begin to pop. Put them in a mortar and grind them to a fine powder with a pestle.

Add chile powder and turmeric and mix well. Sprinkle spice mixture over limes and stir gently. Pour over oil and cover with a dry cloth. Leave in a sunny place 10 to 12 days, until limes have been softened. Pack in sterilized jars, then seal and store in a cool, dark place. Serve at room temperature.

Makes about 6 cups.

Variation: To make lemon pickle, substitute 8 lemons for the limes.

Fresh Mint Relish

8 ounces fresh mint leaves, finely chopped
3 green chiles, seeded, finely chopped
1 small onion, finely chopped
1 (1-inch) piece fresh gingerroot, finely
    chopped
Salt to taste
2 teaspoons superfine sugar
2 tablespoons lemon juice
Mint leaves and lemon slices, to garnish

Put mint leaves, chiles, onion and gingerroot in a bowl and mix thoroughly. Cover and refrigerate at least 1 hour.

Stir in salt, sugar and lemon juice, mixing well. Serve cold, garnished with mint leaves and lemon slices.

Variation: Omit chiles and add 2 tablespoons chopped cilantro instead.

Sautéed Chile Pickle

2 teaspoons sesame seeds
1 teaspoon fennel seeds
2 teaspoons coriander seeds
2 teaspoons cumin seeds
1/4 cup vegetable oil
1/2 teaspoon black peppercorns
20 fresh small green chiles
1 teaspoon mango powder, page 47
3 tablespoons lemon juice
Grated lemon peel, to garnish

Put sesame, fennel, coriander and cumin seeds in a skillet. Dry roast over medium heat, until spices begin to pop.

Add oil, peppercorns, chiles and mango powder and fry, stirring, 3 to 5 minutes, or until chiles are softened. Transfer to a serving dish, sprinkle with lemon juice and cool. Serve at room temperature, garnished with lemon peel.

Note: For a less hot pickle, halve and seed chiles before cooking.

Makes about 4 cups.

Coriander Leaf Chutney

Juice of 2 lemons
1 cup shredded fresh coconut
1 (1-inch) piece fresh gingerroot, grated
1 green chile, seeded
4 ounces cilantro (fresh coriander) leaves
2 green onions, chopped
2 teaspoons sugar
Salt to taste
Cilantro (fresh coriander) leaves and green
  onion brushes, to garnish

Put lemon juice, coconut, gingerroot and chile in a blender or food processor fitted with the metal blade and process until smooth. Spoon into a bowl.

Finely shred cilantro leaves and stir into coconut mixture with green onions, sugar and salt. Cover and refrigerate at least 1 hour. Serve cold, garnished with cilantro leaves and onion brushes.

Makes about 1-1/2 cups.

Note: If fresh coconut is unavailable, substitute the same quantity of dried coconut, soaked in 1/3 cup boiling water 10 minutes, then drained and squeezed to remove excess water.

Eggplant Pickle

1-1/2 lbs. baby eggplants
1/2 teaspoon ground turmeric
Salt to taste
2 cups vegetable oil
6 garlic cloves, crushed
1 (1-inch) piece fresh gingerroot, grated
1 tablespoon Garam Marsala, page 11
1 teaspoon red (cayenne) pepper

Cut eggplants in half lengthwise, sprinkle with turmeric and salt.

Heat 5 tablespoons of oil in a large skillet and fry eggplants about 5 minutes, until golden brown, stirring frequently. Stir in garlic and gingerroot and fry 2 minutes. Stir in Garam Masala, cayenne and remaining oil and cook, uncovered, 10 to 15 minutes, or until eggplants are soft, stirring occasionally.

Cool, then spoon into sterilized jars. Cover jars with a dry cloth 3 days, stirring gently every day. Seal jars and store in a cool, dark place. Serve at room temperature.

Makes about 4 cups.

Note: If baby eggplants are unavailable, use large eggplants and quarter lengthwise, then slice and prepare as above.

Cucumber Raita

1/2 of large cucumber
1 cup plain yogurt
1 tablespoon chopped cilantro (fresh coriander)
1 tablespoon chopped fresh mint
1 green chile, seeded, finely chopped
Salt to taste
1 teaspoon cumin seeds
1 teaspoon mustard seeds
Cilantro (fresh coriander) or mint leaves, to
    garnish

Cut cucumber into matchstick-size pieces and
place in a bowl. Add yogurt, cilantro, mint,
chile and salt; stir gently to mix. Refrigerate
30 minutes.

Meanwhile, put cumin seeds and mustard
seeds in a skillet and dry roast over medium
heat 1 to 2 minutes, until they begin to pop.
Cool, then sprinkle over the yogurt mixture.
Cover and refrigerate 30 minutes. Serve cold,
garnished with cilantro or mint leaves.

Makes about 1-1/2 cups.

Carrot & Pistachio Raita

1/4 cup coarsely chopped pistachios
1/3 cup raisins
6 tablespoons boiling water
4 carrots, coarsely grated
3/4 cup plain yogurt
1 tablespoon chopped fresh mint
1/2 teaspoon chile powder
1/2 teaspoon cardamom seeds, crushed
1/2 teaspoon ground cumin
Salt to taste

Put pistachios and raisins in a small bowl and top with boiling water. Soak 30 minutes, then drain and pat dry with paper towels. Put carrots, yogurt, mint, chile powder, cardamom seeds, cumin and salt in a bowl and stir to mix.

Cover and refrigerate 30 minutes. Stir all but 2 tablespoons of pistachios and raisins into yogurt, then sprinkle remainder on top. Serve cold.

Makes about 1-1/2 cups.

Variation: Substitute chopped blanched almonds for pistachios.

Beet Yogurt Salad

6 cooked baby beets
1 cup plain yogurt
1 teaspoon sugar
Salt and red (cayenne) pepper to taste
1 tablespoon snipped fresh chives
Small bunch of chives, to garnish

Cut beets into 1/8-inch-thick slices and arrange on a serving plate. Cover and refrigerate 30 minutes. Put yogurt into a bowl and stir in sugar, salt and cayenne. Cover and refrigerate 30 minutes.

Pour yogurt mixture over beets and sprinkle with chives. Serve cold, garnished with chives.

Makes 4 to 6 servings.

Variation: Or, dice beets and stir into yogurt before chilling.

Cucumber & Chiles

8 ounces cucumber
Salt to taste
2 green chiles, seeded, finely sliced
1 small fresh red chile, seeded, finely chopped
2 tablespoons white wine vinegar
1 teaspoon superfine sugar

Very thinly slice cucumber. Place in a colander and sprinkle with salt. Drain 30 minutes, then rinse thoroughly under cold running water. Pat dry with paper towels and arrange on a serving plate.

Sprinkle chiles over cucumber. Put vinegar and sugar in a small bowl and mix well. Sprinkle over cucumber, then cover and refrigerate 30 minutes. Serve cold.

Note: The chile seeds can be left in, if preferred, to make the dish very hot.

Tomato Kuchumber

12 ounces cherry tomatoes
6 green onions
1 green chile, seeded, chopped
1 tablespoon lemon juice
Salt and red (cayenne) pepper to taste
2 tablespoons chopped cilantro (fresh coriander)
Green onions, to garnish

Quarter tomatoes and put in a serving bowl. Cut onions diagonally into long, thin slices. Scatter onions and chile over tomatoes and gently mix together.

Sprinkle vegetables with lemon juice, salt, cayenne and cilantro, then cover and refrigerate 30 minutes. Serve cold, garnished with green onions.

Makes 4 to 6 servings.

Variation: Use larger tomatoes, if preferred, slice thinly and arrange on a serving plate. Scatter other ingredients over top, before chilling.

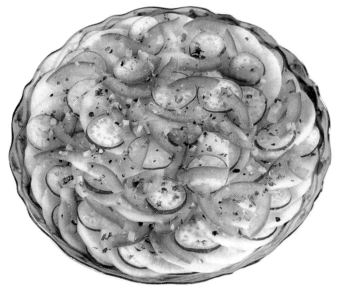

White & Red Radish Salad

6 ounces white radish
10 red radishes
1 small green bell pepper
1 green chile, seeded, finely chopped
2 tablespoons lime juice
Salt to taste
6 black peppercorns, coarsely ground
1 tablespoon chopped fresh mint

Peel and thinly slice white radish and slice red radishes. Arrange on a serving plate. Cut pepper into six pieces lengthwise, remove seeds and stem and slice finely. Scatter bell pepper and chile over radishes. Sprinkle salad with lime juice, salt, peppercorns and mint. Cover and refrigerate 30 minutes. Serve cold.

Makes 4 to 6 servings.

Chapati

1-1/4 cups all-purpose flour
1-1/4 cups whole-wheat flour
Salt to taste
About 3/4 cup water
1/4 cup butter or ghee, melted, plus extra for
    serving

Sift together flours and salt into a medium bowl, add any bran remaining in sifter. Mix in enough water to make a soft dough.

Knead dough on a lightly floured surface about 5 minutes, until smooth and pliable, then with wet hands, knead dough 1 minute more to make it extra smooth. Wrap in plastic wrap; refrigerate 30 minutes. Divide dough into 12 pieces and roll each out on a lightly floured surface to a 5-inch round.

Heat a griddle or heavy skillet over medium heat; cook rounds one at a time, floured side down, 1 to 2 minutes, until beginning to bubble on surface. Turn over and cook 30 to 60 seconds, pressing with a folded dry cloth during cooking to make them puff up. Wrap chapatis in a dry cloth as they are ready. Serve warm, brushed with extra melted butter.

Makes 12.

Naan

4 cups all-purpose flour
1 teaspoon baking powder
1/2 teaspoon baking soda
Salt to taste
1 egg, beaten
6 tablespoons plain yogurt
3 tablespoons butter or ghee, melted
About 1 cup milk
1 tablespoon poppy seeds

Sift together flour, baking powder, baking soda and salt into a medium bowl.

Stir in egg, yogurt and 2 tablespoons butter. Gradually mix in enough milk to make a soft dough. Cover bowl with a damp cloth and put in a warm place 2 hours. Preheat oven to 400F (205C). Knead dough on a lightly floured surface for 2 to 3 minutes until smooth, then divide dough into 8 pieces.

Roll each piece into a ball, then roll out to make ovals about 6 inches long, pulling ends to stretch dough into shape. Brush ovals with water and place wet side down on greased baking sheets. Brush dry side with melted butter; sprinkle with poppy seeds. Bake 8 to 10 minutes, until puffy and golden brown.

Makes 8.

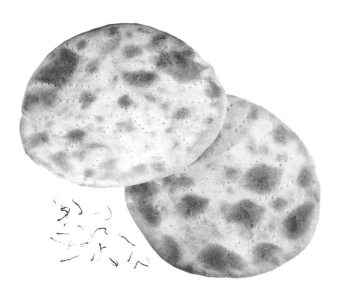

Flaky Oven Bread

4 cups all-purpose flour
Salt to taste
1/2 cup butter or ghee, chilled
2 teaspoons superfine sugar
2 cups milk
Pinch of saffron threads

Sift together flour and salt into a medium bowl. Cut in all but 1 tablespoon of the butter, until mixture resembles coarse crumbs. Stir in sugar, then add about 1-1/4 cups milk to make a soft dough.

Knead dough until smooth, then put into a clean, lightly oiled bowl. Cover and put in a cool place 2 hours. Put remaining milk in a small pan and heat until almost boiling, add saffron threads and let soak 1-1/2 to 2 hours. Preheat oven to 450F (230C); place a heavy baking sheet in oven to heat. Knead dough on a lightly floured surface and divide into 8 pieces. Roll 4 pieces at a time into balls, keeping rest covered with a dry cloth.

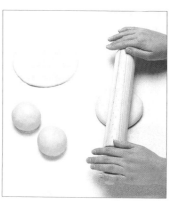

Flatten and roll first 4 balls out to 6-inch rounds. Prick all over with a fork. Press onto heated baking sheet in oven. Bake about 8 minutes, until beginning to brown, sprinkling rounds with a little saffron milk twice—without removing them from oven. Melt remaining butter or ghee and brush over breads, then sandwich them buttered sides together and wrap in a dry cloth while preparing remaining rounds. Serve warm.

Makes 8.

Parathas

1/2 cup all-purpose flour
2/3 cup whole-wheat flour
Salt to taste
1/2 teaspoon onion seeds
1/2 teaspoon celery seeds
About 2/3 cup water
1 cup butter or ghee, melted
Celery leaves, to garnish

Sift together flours and salt into a medium bowl; add any bran remaining in sifter. Stir in onion and celery seeds, then mix in enough water to form a fairly soft dough.

Knead dough on a lightly floured surface 5 minutes, or until pliable and smooth. Wrap in plastic wrap; refrigerate 30 minutes. Divide dough into 10 pieces and roll each out to a 5-inch round. Brush one side of each round with butter, then fold in half with buttered side inside. Brush top side with butter and fold in half again to make a triangle.

Roll out triangles on a lightly floured surface until both straight sides measure about 5 inches. Heat a griddle or heavy skillet and brush with butter. Cook 2 or 3 parathas at a time 1 minute, brush with butter, then turn over and cook 1 to 2 minutes more, until cooked. Stack on a plate, cover with a dry cloth while cooking remaining bread. Serve warm, garnished with celery leaves.

Makes 10.

Poori

1/3 cup all-purpose flour
1/3 cup whole-wheat flour
Pinch of salt
1/4 teaspoon cardamom seeds
About 2 tablespoons vegetable oil plus extra for
    deep-frying
About 1/4 cup warm water

Sift flours and salt into a medium bowl; add any bran remaining in sifter. Stir in cardamom seeds and 1 tablespoon oil; mix in enough of the water to make a soft dough.

Knead dough 5 minutes on a lightly oiled surface, with a little oil rubbed into hands to prevent them from sticking, until dough is soft and pliable. Cover with plastic wrap and let rest 10 minutes. Divide dough into 8 pieces; roll into balls. Dust balls with flour and cover with a damp cloth. Roll each ball out to a 3-inch round, keeping unrolled balls and finished rounds covered with a cloth.

Half-fill a deep pan or deep-fryer with oil and heat to 375F (190C) or until a 1-inch bread cube browns in 50 seconds. Fry poori one at a time, turning over once, 30 to 60 seconds. Keep patting top of pooris gently with a slotted spoon as they cook to make them puff up. Serve at once.

Makes 8.

Dosa

1/3 cup urad dhal or brown lentils
1 cup long-grain rice
12 tablespoons water
2 green onions, finely chopped
2 tablespoons chopped cilantro (fresh
   coriander)
1 (1-inch) piece fresh gingerroot, grated
1 green chile, seeded, chopped
1/2 teaspoon salt
About 3 tablespoons water
Vegetable oil
Cilantro (fresh coriander) leaves, to garnish

Wash dhal and rice thoroughly; put into separate bowls. Add 2 cups water to each; soak 3 hours, then drain well.

Put dhal in a blender or food processor fitted with the metal blade. Add 6 tablespoons water and process until smooth. Puree rice with 6 tablespoons water in same way. Mix purees together in a large bowl, cover with a damp cloth and set aside at room temperature about 12 hours.

Stir in onions, cilantro, gingerroot, chile, salt and enough water to make a thin batter. Heat a 6-inch skillet over high heat, brush with a little oil, then pour in 2 to 3 tablespoons batter and spread into a 4-inch circle. Cook about 3 minutes, until browned, turning over after about 1-1/2 minutes. Stack on a plate; cover with a dry cloth, while cooking remaining bread. Serve warm, garnished with cilantro leaves.

Makes about 12.

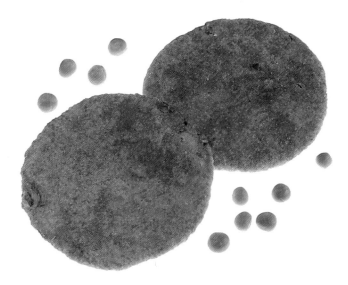

Green Pea Kachori

4 cups whole-wheat flour
About 1/4 cup water
1/4 teaspoon salt
1/2 teaspoon cumin seeds
1/2 teaspoon anise seeds
2 tablespoons vegetable oil plus extra for
    deep-frying
1 green chile, seeded, chopped
1 (1-inch) piece fresh gingerroot, grated
1/4 cup frozen green peas, thawed

Sift flour and salt into a medium bowl, add any bran remaining in sifter. Mix in enough water to make a soft dough. Knead on a lightly floured surface 5 minutes.

Set dough aside, covered with a dry cloth. Heat a skillet over medium heat; add cumin seeds and anise seeds, dry fry 30 to 60 seconds, until beginning to pop, then grind with a mortar and pestle. Heat oil in pan, add ground spices, chile and gingerroot and cook for 2 minutes. Mash peas, then add to pan and cook 1 minute more. Cool completely. Divide dough into 12 pieces and roll into balls.

Make a depression in each, press in about 1 teaspoon filling and smooth over dough to seal. Roll each ball out on a lightly floured surface to a 3-inch round. Half-fill a deep pan or deep-fryer with oil and heat to 375F (190C) or until a 1-inch cube of bread browns in 50 seconds. Fry two kachori at a time 2 to 3 minutes, or until golden brown. Serve warm.

Makes 12.

Nimki

1 cup all-purpose flour
1/2 teaspoon salt
1 tablespoon butter or ghee, chilled
Large pinch of chile powder
1/4 teaspoon superfine sugar
1/2 teaspoon onion seeds
About 4 tablespoons water
Vegetable oil for deep-frying
Chile flowers, to garnish, if desired

Sift together flour and salt into a medium bowl. Cut in butter until mixture resembles coarse crumbs.

Stir in chile powder, sugar and onion seeds, then mix in enough water to make a soft dough. Roll out dough on a floured surface to a thickness of 1/8 inch. Prick all over with a fork and cut into 1-inch strips. Cut strips diagonally to make about 30 diamond shapes.

Half-fill a deep pan or deep-fryer with oil and heat to 350F (190C) or until a 1-inch cube of bread browns in 50 seconds. Fry nimkis in two or three batches 1 to 2 minutes, until crisp and golden brown. Drain on paper towels and cool. Serve, garnished with chile flowers, if desired.

Makes about 30.

Note: These tiny crisp breads are ideal for party nibbles. Make them a day or two in advance and store in an airtight container.

Banana Yogurt Milkshake

4 ripe bananas
1/3 cup brown sugar
1 teaspoon cardamom seeds
3-3/4 cups cold milk
2/3 cup plain yogurt
6 ice cubes

Peel and slice bananas; reserve a few slices for decoration. Put remainder in a blender or food processor fitted with the metal blade; add sugar, cardamom seeds, milk, yogurt and ice cubes. Process until smooth and very frothy.

Pour into tall glasses and decorate with reserved banana slices. Serve at once, with straws.

Makes about 5 cups.

Milk & Saffron Drink

1/2 teaspoon saffron threads
2 tablespoons boiling water
1/3 cup shelled pistachio nuts
Seeds from 10 green cardamom pods
1/4 cup superfine sugar
5 cups cold milk
Crushed ice
1/4 cup chopped pistachio nuts

Put saffron and boiling water in a small bowl; soak 30 minutes. Put in a blender or food processor fitted with the metal blade; add pistachio nuts, cardamom seeds and sugar. Process until smooth. Add milk and process until frothy.

Half-fill glasses with ice and pour in frothy milk mixture. Sprinkle with chopped pistachio nuts and serve at once.

Makes about 5 cups.

Orange Drink

About 8 oranges
1/2 cup superfine sugar
1-1/2 cups plain water
Ice cubes
2-1/2 cups sparkling mineral water
Orange peel spirals and mint sprigs, to
    decorate

Squeeze juice from oranges to make 2-1/2 cups juice. Meanwhile, put sugar and plain water in a large saucepan; cook over a low heat, stirring occasionally, until sugar dissolves. Boil 5 minutes. Add orange juice and simmer another 5 minutes. Cool, then chill.

To serve, put ice cubes in glasses, add a little orange syrup, top with mineral water and decorate with orange peel and mint sprigs.

Makes about 5 cups.

Note: Use 2-1/2 cups commercial freshly squeezed orange juice, if preferred.

Mango Milkshake

4 large ripe mangoes
1/3 cup superfine sugar
3 cups cold milk
Crushed ice

Peel and seed mangoes. Put flesh in a blender or food processor fitted with the metal blade; process until smooth. Add sugar and milk; process until frothy.

Half-fill glasses with crushed ice; pour milk mixture over ice. Serve at once, with straws.

Makes about 5 cups.

Note: If your blender or processor is small, process in two batches.

Fragrant Lemon Drink

Grated peel and juice of 2 lemons
1/4 cup superfine sugar
1 cup packed lemon balm leaves
Crushed ice
About 4 cups iced water
Lemon peel and lemon balm leaves, to decorate

Put lemon peel and juice, sugar and lemon balm leaves in a blender or food processor fitted with the metal blade; process until smooth. Strain into a pitcher and chill.

Fill glasses with crushed ice, add a little lemon concentrate and top with iced water, to taste. Serve at once, decorated with lemon peel and lemon balm leaves.

Makes about 5 cups.

Note: Lemon peel spirals: cut a long strip of peel from a lemon using a zester. Wind strip of peel around a skewer or chopstick, fasten securely to prevent it from unwinding and blanch in boiling water a few seconds. Rinse in cold water and remove skewer.

Spiced Tea

1 tablespoon plus 2 teaspoons black
    peppercorns
1 tablespoon cardamom seeds
1 tablespoon whole cloves
1 (1-1/2-inch) cinnamon stick
1/3 cup ground ginger
Hot tea
Boiling water
Milk and sugar to taste

Put peppercorns, cardamom seeds, cloves and cinnamon in a mortar and grind to a fine powder with a pestle. Add ginger and grind again a few seconds to mix. Add about 1/2 teaspoon of spice mixture to a pot of tea; leave in a warm place 1 to 2 minutes to brew. Serve hot, with milk and sugar.

Makes about 8 tablespoons spice mix, enough for 16 pots of tea.

Note: Store remaining spice mixture in an airtight container, in a dark cupboard to preserve its flavor. It will keep 2 to 3 months.

Lime & Mint Drink

6 tablespoons lime juice
1/4 cup superfine sugar
Pinch of salt
1 cup packed mint leaves
Ice cubes
About 4 cups iced water
Lime slices and mint leaves, to decorate

Pour lime juice into a blender or food processor fitted with the metal blade. Add sugar, salt and mint leaves; process until smooth. Strain into a pitcher, cover and refrigerate until cold.

Half-fill tall glasses with ice cubes; add a little lime juice concentrate and top with iced water to taste. Serve at once, decorated with lime slices and mint leaves.

Makes about 5 cups.

Indian Summer Punch

1 tablespoon fennel seeds
Seeds from 6 green cardamom pods
3 whole cloves
4 black peppercorns
1/2 cup ground almonds
1/4 cup shelled pistachio nuts
1/2 cup shelled sunflower seeds
1-1/4 cups boiling water
1/2 cup superfine sugar
3 cups cold milk
pple slices and fennel sprigs, to decorate

Put fennel seeds, cardamom seeds, cloves and peppercorns in a mortar and grind to a fine powder with a pestle.

Put almonds, pistachios and sunflower seeds in a small bowl; add 6 tablespoons of the boiling water. Soak 20 minutes, then drain. Put in a blender or food processor fitted with the metal blade; add remaining boiling water and process until smooth.

Add spices and sugar; process again. Strain through a cheesecloth, squeezing paste to extract as much liquid as possible. Discard paste, cover and refrigerate liquid at least 1 hour, then mix with milk and serve in tall glasses over ice, decorated with apple slices and fennel sprigs.

Makes about 6 cups.

Note: If preferred, grind spices in a coffee grinder.

— INDEX —